Marriage Counseling

2 in 1

How To Save Your Marriage from Divorce With The Power Of Effective Communication

SHIRLEY COLE

Copyright 2019 © Shirley Cole

All rights reserved.

No part of this guide may be reproduced in any form without permission in writing from the publisher except in the case of review.

Legal & Disclaimer

The following document is reproduced below with the goal of providing information that is as accurate and reliable as possible.

This declaration is deemed fair and valid by both the American Bar Association and the Committee of Publishers Association and is legally binding throughout the United States.

Furthermore, the transmission, duplication or reproduction of any of the following work including specific information will be considered an illegal act irrespective of if it is done electronically or in print. This extends to creating a secondary or tertiary copy of the work or a recorded copy and is only allowed with an express written consent from the Publisher. All additional right reserved.

The information in the following pages is broadly considered to be a truthful and accurate account of facts, and as such any inattention, use or misuse of the information in question by the reader will render any resulting actions solely under their purview. There are no scenarios in which the publisher or the original author of this work can be in any fashion deemed liable for any hardship or damages that may befall them after undertaking information described herein.

Additionally, the information in the following pages is intended only for informational purposes and should thus be thought of as universal. As befitting its nature, it is presented without assurance regarding its prolonged validity or interim quality. Trademarks that are mentioned are done without written consent and can in no way be considered an endorsement from the trademark holder.

Table of Contents

Book 1: Save Your Marriage 7

Introduction 8

Chapter One: Improving Communication 18

Chapter Two: Making Marriage Work 45

Chapter Three: Dealing With Porn Addiction 82

Chapter Four: Rebuilding Broken Trust 96

Chapter Five: Dead Bedrooms 125

Chapter Six: Handling Emotional Abuse 139

Chapter Seven: Saving Your Marriage 150

Chapter Eight: Divorce 182

Final Words 206

Book 2: Communication In Marriage 213

Introduction 214

Chapter One: Communicate Styles and What Our Bodies are Saying 226

Chapter Two: Building Your Communication Toolbox 274

Chapter Three: The Key To a Healthy And Lifelong Marriage: Trust 319

Chapter Four: Keeping Your Marriage A.L.I.V.E. and Staying in Love 360

Chapter Five: 10 Ways to Successfully Destroy a Marriage (and How to Bring it Back from the Brink of Divorce) 393

Chapter Six: ACTION PLAN For Positive Communication In Marriage 422

Final Words 435

References 444

Book 1:
Save Your Marriage

How To Rebuild Broken Trust And Reconnect With Your Spouse No Matter How Far Apart You've Drifted

Introduction

Having to navigate the murky, confusing world of relationships is one of the trickier aspects of being human. Any relationship can be difficult, but romantic relationships are the most confusing and hardest to handle of all. When it comes to romantic relationships, it doesn't get much harder than marriage. When you swear vows to another person that are meant to last until death or divorce, you enter into a formal bond with that person. Regardless of the relationship you had before or the time you've already spent together, getting married changes things significantly. Ending a marriage is not a relatively simple task like breaking up with someone, but a complicated and lengthy legal procedure. When you get married, the whole nature and atmosphere of the relationship you have with your partner changes. Suddenly, things are far more committed and serious, even though nothing physical has changed. You both still look the same, sound the same, even feel the same as you did when you were dating or engaged. What has changed is your attitude and mindset, along with that of your spouse. It's a subtle change, one that you might not even notice at first, but it's there. You're both in it for the long haul now, is the thinking: for better or worse.

When you get married, you undertake a different stage in the journey you're on with your partner. There is far more expectation placed upon the relationship by both you and your friends and family. People talk about you differently and make references to the fact that you're now married. Again, the effect is subtle and the change often unnoticeable. After all, you might tell yourself, you're still the same couple you've always been. If anything, you can only be more in love now, right? Things can only get better from here because you're legally bound to one another. While marriage is certainly a beautiful and fulfilling experience, it can and does add a certain extra level of strain to things. Particularly as after you get married, you're statistically more likely to consider buying a house, have children, and look for more challenge and financial reward from your job. The strain created by being married and all the life development that comes with it can put you under an immense amount of pressure. It also has a nasty habit of bringing to light other difficulties in your relationship and personal lives as a result. This is why the divorce rate approaches fifty percent of all marriages. Making a marriage go the distance is a very hard thing to do.

In the not so distant past, divorce was not a common occurrence like it is today. In fact, it was very difficult to get a divorce at all unless you had a satisfactory reason. The culture of the time was that once a couple married, they stuck together through thick and thin. Of course, this didn't mean that people simply forced themselves to be happy — miserable married couples have always been a common occurrence — but they found a way to make it work. These days, the comparative ease of getting a divorce has seen divorce rates skyrocket. People are often quick to blame their spouses for the problems in their life and relationship, and can easily convince themselves that the grass could be greener with someone else. Often, though, people who remarry are even more likely to divorce again. At some point, you have to stop blaming your partner, look in the mirror, and take full stock of the reasons why your marriage isn't working. The alternative to doing this is a lifetime of failed relationships and miserable marriages.

If your marriage is broken and doesn't make either you or your spouse happy, it's a one-way road. Sooner or later, you're headed for divorce. The problems you face won't just go away of their own accord. Working through such issues is a matter of being able to change the way you view them in the first place. Throughout my career as a professional therapist, I've seen the same problems over and over again. When I meet the vast majority of my married, counseling-seeking clients for the first time, fixing the issues in their relationship and saving their marriage is their main priority, but it's something that feels perpetually out of reach. There's always another argument, another flashpoint for conflict and another fight. Sometimes there's been lying and infidelity, so perhaps the trust they shared is gone. Their marriage is on the rocks, and they're looking for a way to save it. My role is to step in and try to alter the way they view their marriage, their problems, and themselves.

It's not enough to just help a couple stay together, however. There's no point in convincing someone not to get divorced if they're going to live a life of misery instead. There are a lot of married couples out there who do just that; they stay together, miserable, rather than seeking happiness apart. Not only does their marriage need to be saved in such cases, but it needs to be overhauled and changed. The love and passion need to return. If a couple's sex life is AWOL, it needs to be found. In order to save your marriage, you need to not only stay together but be happy together. You need to be fulfilled, you need to want to be together, and you need to break new ground and rediscover the intimacy in your relationship. Through the techniques in this book, all that is possible. Not every marriage can be saved, but all that is required to save any marriage is the willingness to do what is required to make things work. That's it. That's all it comes down to. If both parties are willing to put forth the effort, there is no obstacle too tall for you to climb. There's no mountain you can't summit together.

Throughout my career as a professional therapist, I've built up a great deal of experience in making things work between married couples. I've seen it all. There is nothing that can shock me. I've seen closets with more skeletons than clothes and much, much more. One thing I've learned from all of this experience is that there's no such thing as a marriage without hope of getting better. Sure, sometimes there are two people with no desire to make it work — but in these cases, there's nothing left to save. When neither person wants to take the action required to fix things, there's nothing to be done. When it comes to the circumstances themselves, however, there is no set of events too difficult or too tough to move past when both people are willing to do what is necessary to make things work. I've coached couples who thought their relationship was far beyond repair return to being happy, mutually appreciating, and loving partners. I've seen spouses with the worst track records imaginable go on to be fulfilled and satisfied with their marriage. If they can make it work, you can too.

Saving your marriage is about embracing a new lease of life. You enter into a new stage in your relationship with your spouse, where you let the past be the past and focus on living well in the present and creating a better future. With this book, you'll be able to leave the petty bickering, arguments, and bad feelings behind and instead enter a new way of being together. It will help you focus on the joy in your life, rather than the misery. It will allow you to look at things more positively and show you that attitude is everything when it comes to making a marriage go the distance. It represents the culmination of my fifteen years of experience as a professional family therapist and is the sum total of the advice and expertise I offer to my clients. Over the course of my career, I've successfully coached hundreds of married couples on how to save, improve, and overhaul their marriage to stop the rot of a miserable coexistence and embrace the beauty of sharing a long, happy, intimate bond with each other that lasts them the rest of their lives.

This book contains the information you need to save your marriage. It will teach you the attitude and mindset that you need to cultivate to make things work with your spouse and change your marriage for the better. If you want to turn things around and embrace a better, happier marriage and a more fulfilling life, then read this book and get started on your journey to peace and joy. I promise you that if saving your marriage is what you want to do, then this book will equip you with the tools you need to not only rescue your marriage and uphold your vows, but to reinvent the nature of your relationship with your spouse completely. So, what are you waiting for? There's no point in spending any more time living a life that isn't satisfying or fulfilling. Break the cycle of misery now and by reading this book and finding out how to save your marriage!

Chapter One:
Improving Communication

We all know how to communicate. It's one of the most fundamental components of being human. We don't all know how to communicate well, however. There's no place where good, positive communication is more essential than in a relationship. It can make all the difference when it comes to cultivating a positive, joyful, loving marriage. In this chapter, I'll be taking you through why great communication is so vital and how to implement it in your relationship with your spouse to make a real difference.

The Importance of Good Communication

Communication is about a message being transferred between two individuals, a sender and a receiver, or speaker and listener. We encode information via language and transmit it to be decoded by someone else in order for them to decipher our meaning. Through this process, we can deliver insight into the internal worlds we experience and work to better understand one another, as well as deepening our knowledge of ourselves; speaking is a part of thought, and we have to talk to understand how we truly think about something. This is why we all have internal monologues of thought where we 'speak' to ourselves with words.

Communication is a skill. When we're good at practicing it, we're more effective at the whole process of sending and receiving messages. The more skilled we are in communication, the better we're able to explain what we mean and understand what other people are trying to tell us. Although most of us probably like to consider ourselves good communicators, the truth is that communication is relatively simple to do but very difficult to do well. The result is that most of the communication that takes place in our relationships and everyday life is incredibly inefficient. Both physical and mental noise along with other distractions can make the listener's job very hard and stop them from focusing on or otherwise listening to the words being said, resulting in a lot of meaning being simply lost in translation.

When it comes to marriage, being able to communicate well is vitally important. Any long-term romantic relationship represents an immense amount of time spent together and a very close level of interaction — in a marriage, this is amplified tenfold. Spending such a great deal of time with another person in overwhelmingly close proximity with so much at stake always leads to conflict and problems. When we spend enough time with anyone, we inevitably come to be annoyed by aspects of their being. The same is even true for becoming annoyed with yourself after spending too much time alone. Even couples that are very much alike will have vast differences in areas of their personality and preferences, leading to a range of issues from mildly irritating all the way to argument-causing, divorce-heralding ones. It's no wonder there's so much conflict in marriages. They're perfect, fertile breeding grounds for it.

The thing is, every person and every marriage has problems. In fact, roughly 70% of all conflict-causing problems in marriages are seen as unresolvable by both spouses; interestingly, this applies to marriages that are healthy, happy, and mutually fulfilling, as well as those that are burning down and heading for divorce. This shows us that conflict, problems, and issues in relationships are simply part of being human, and a marriage is no exception to this. There will always be issues and opportunities for conflict.

No one is perfect. What's really important, then, is the attitude that we take about these problems. A good marriage, a bad marriage, it doesn't matter — both have problems. It's the mindset and approach that we take to these problems that determine how good our relationship is, not the circumstances that cause the problems themselves. Having a happy marriage is about doing more of what works, and less of what doesn't — and good communication works better than anything else. Great, positive communication can make all the difference in your marriage, allowing you to work through issues that might otherwise derail things.

they already know exactly what they're going to do. They just want their spouses to validate how they feel.

Men, however, are far less likely to feel like they have to express themselves and be open about what goes on in their hearts and minds. They also tend to be conditioned by their culture and upbringing into believing that it's emasculating to express their feelings or talk about how they feel. A lot of men still buy into the idea that men shouldn't cry or show any form of weakness, and instead simply bottle up how they feel rather than getting it off of their chests.

Love Languages

Another difference in communication that's worth mentioning here is love languages. In a 1992 book called The Five Love Languages: How to Express Heartfelt Commitment to Your Mate, author Gary Chapman proposed that different people mainly express their love in one of five different ways. This can lead to confusion and hurt when half of a couple expresses their feelings of affection and love differently than the other. For example, one person might use words of affirmation in order to express their love, whereas the other may instead rely on physical touch to convey the way they feel to their partner. The end result is that neither person feels fully loved or fulfilled because they're both sending the right signals in completely different ways. The messages end up going over each other's heads because they're expecting to receive love in the same way that they express it.

There are widely thought to be five different love languages, as initially proposed by Chapman and verified by millions of couples ever since:

1. **Words of affirmation:** These are the spoken words we use to declare our love for our partners, such as telling them how much they mean to us, how much we love them, and how grateful we are to have them in our lives.

2. **Physical touch:** This refers to any physical or intimate contact we have with our spouse, like holding their hand, cuddling, and kissing them on the cheek.

3. **Quality time:** This is the time we take out of our lives to dedicate to being with our partner, enjoying their company and getting to know them better.

4. **Gift giving:** This is the giving of presents and gifts, and can mean anything from small symbols of love like making coffee or breakfast to paying for vacations and jewelry.

It's about the little thoughtful things we do for each other.

5. **Acts of service:** This refers to those things we do for our partners to show them we love them and that we care by standing by them and helping them out. It can mean things as little as giving them a ride somewhere or larger things like helping them out when they're in a tight spot financially or assisting them with a project they're working on just because we can and we want to.

If you can work out what your own primary love language is, as well as that of your spouse, you may well be able to better communicate your love and affection to one another by doing more to express your feelings in your partner's love language. You can also learn to better understand your partner's expressions of love by becoming more aware of when they're trying to show you they love you.

How To Communicate Well

When we're involved in the process of communicating with someone, we have one of two roles: we're either speaking or listening.

Speaking

Good communication is about understanding each of these roles and being able to practice them well regardless of the situation you're in or which one you need to use. When you're speaking, you need to keep in mind that you are first expressing to be understood. That is your main goal and priority — it should, therefore, be your primary concern, rather than speaking to persuade or to influence or inform. All of that is secondary. Speaking to be understood means focusing on getting an accurate representation of the message you want to send that is held in your mind across to the listener in such a way as to minimize miscommunication and misunderstanding. Your objective is to send 'A' and have the listener receive 'A' rather than 'B'.

When we communicate, we encode a message or meaning, in a language to transmit it to a receiver who then decodes the message to understand the meaning for themselves. The language we use influences how well this message is transmitted to our audience. Being an effective communicator when it comes to speaking is about choosing our language in a way that makes it easy to understand for our audience: the listener, whoever that is at the time. For example, if you were speaking to a child, you'd use simpler, less complicated language than if you were talking to a fellow professional in your line of work, in which case you'd use more specialized language to better make your point.

When you're talking to your spouse, you should try to express yourself as well as you can in order to make them understand where you're coming from. This is important in everyday situations like going to the grocery store or picking the kids up from school, but it's especially important when it comes to having difficult conversations where emotions are surfacing and you have to be vulnerable. Marriage is as intimate a relationship as it gets, and each of you needs to be able to open up to each other completely to make things work. If you feel like you can't be totally open and honest about the way you feel, then say so. At least be honest about that. Through simple heartfelt discussion and speaking the truth, a lot of progress can be made. Many married couples that have issues they feel just can't be resolved — when the fact of the matter is that they don't open up to each other honestly enough to even begin to resolve them in the first place. Marriage is hard, and talking about how you feel and why you feel the way you do is hard, too, but it has to happen. You should feel like you can talk about absolutely anything with your spouse, and they with you.

Listening

For most people, speaking is the easier half of the communication process. By its very nature, speaking is an active process. When we're talking, we're doing something proactive and creative. We work out what points we want to express in our minds and then put them into words in an ongoing process. Sentences flow together to convey meaning to our audience. Most of us can quite easily get into the zone when talking. It's only when we're distracted or run out of things to say or the right words to say something, that talking becomes more difficult.

When it comes to listening, however, things can be much more challenging.

Listening is a more passive process, as we're not constructing or encoding meaning but rather decoding it. While we still have to actively listen, we can easily switch off or become distracted without it being clear that we've done so. It's far more challenging to listen effectively because we have to pay complete attention to what is being said. We can't properly listen to what someone is saying and do anything else at the same time. We get distracted, and then we end up missing out on the information that is being transmitted, resulting in miscommunication and misunderstanding.

Practicing effective communication as a listener is all about understanding the message the speaker is trying to transmit to you. Agreeing with them isn't the goal here; you should instead simply desire to understand. Focus on your job, and make sure that what the speaker intends to communicate is the message that you receive. When you're listening, your job is to listen, so do your best to not interrupt unless it's to ask for clarification about something the speaker has said. You should also do your best to avoid thinking about rebuttals or responses while you're listening, as this will distract you and stop you from listening intently. A great way to be an effective listener, especially in one-on-one conversations like a talk between you and your spouse, is to practice reflective listening. This is a process where as you listen, you provide the speaker with indications that you're listening such as positive and affirmative vocalizations, head nods, and a good level of eye contact. You can then 'reflect' back your understanding of what the speaker has said to them in order for them to make sure it matches the meaning of their original message.

Many people are of the opinion that they listen well to their spouse when in reality they only listen as far as they allow their spouse to speak. Rather than giving their partner as much time and space as they need to express themselves, they will often take opportunities to cut them short to weigh in with their own opinion. Listening to your spouse when they talk is about validating their feelings regardless of whether you agree with how they feel about something. Your opinion on the matter is more or less irrelevant. It won't change how they feel. They feel how they feel, and the best way to work through difficult issues and troubling emotions is to simply let them feel it. You have to be patient, open and receptive to the way your spouse feels, no matter how you might feel about it. If they don't feel like you give them an open and non-judgmental forum for them to express themselves fully, they will only bottle up their emotions and end up resenting you. If listening hasn't been your strong suit in the past, make an effort to change that now by shutting up and paying attention to your spouse when they tell you how they feel. Encourage them to open up; tell them that you want to understand them better by just listening as they pour their heart out to you. Set aside any desire you may have to control how they feel or what they think or say. Simply let your partner be free to be themselves, and accept whatever they tell you without judgment and with an open mind. Be patient by allowing them to speak with complete freedom and at their own pace.

Learning to listen to your spouse properly represents a quantum leap in your relationship and marriage. By giving them space and time to fully express themselves, they will probably be motivated to reciprocate and return the favor for you. Establishing a culture of openness, freedom of expression, and emotional security in your marriage in this way lays the groundwork for dealing with past, current, and future problems alike in a way that is mature, calm, and empathetic. Listening to people helps you to understand them better. The reasons they are the way they are, the little thoughts behind their actions, and the feelings behind their words become clearer. It helps you to genuinely put yourself in their shoes and see things from their perspective, a skill that might as well be a superpower when it comes to managing your relationships with people. Listening might not be the single key to saving your marriage, but it's an important first step.

Body Language

When it comes to face-to-face communication, many people tend to assume that speaking and listening makes up the bulk of it. In fact, the majority of communication in interpersonal interaction is nonverbal. Some researchers and behavioral psychologists even think it might be as much as 90%! When we speak or even listen, we're not talking only with our words. Our bodies automatically broadcast messages about how we feel and what we think. This is a mostly subconscious process, although we can control it when we pay attention to it for as long as we pay attention to it — much like breathing. On the whole, however, our body language is something that happens without us even noticing we're doing it, meaning it can often betray our true feelings when we're trying our best to put on a front with our words.

These subtle indicators of our true internal feelings manifest themselves in a variety of ways; our posture, the way we carry and hold ourselves, what we do with our hands or our legs, and our facial expressions all give clues to what state of mind we're in and how we feel about a particular situation. For example, having our arms crossed is defensive body language, and suggests a person feels uncomfortable or on edge. Likewise, having our hands by our sides or using them animatedly when we're speaking suggests a more open and expressive mood. Additionally, our tone of voice and eye contact also give away signs of our internal makeup. Our body language is usually interpreted by others on a subconscious and automatic level. While it's not something we tend to notice or think about consciously, our minds nevertheless pick up on it and note what another person's body language is broadcasting. This manifests itself as a gut feeling we get about someone; we can pick up on when someone is angry or upset relatively easily, just because of the body language they're giving off — although we might not even think about how we know.

Body language is a very instinctual and primitive form of communication. It's what most animals rely on to communicate in the wild, even ones with complex social groups and complicated interactions such as our fellow great apes or dogs and cats. Although we might like to think of ourselves as highly evolved and educated, relying on our words rather than our bodies, we're still highly tuned in and sensitive to body language. We not only pick up on the body language of other people, but we trust what it's telling us more than we trust the words they're saying. This is why we can pick up on sarcasm pretty easily. When the message of someone's words doesn't match their tone of voice or their body language, we disregard the words and use their behavior and tone to judge their true feelings. We also tend to mirror other people's body language when we're interacting with or otherwise paying attention to them, without noticing we're doing it. Next time you're in a group meeting, cross your arms and lean back in your chair, and then notice other people doing it too over the next few minutes. Mirroring body language in this way is an instinctive way of promoting social cohesion and synchronizing mood in order for us to better fit in with the people around us.

Mirroring can also be reverse engineered in a way to read what another person's body is saying. When you notice someone's body language but are struggling to work out what it's saying about their inner being, you can mimic it at a later point when you're alone and see what kind of feelings a certain behavior gives you. Through doing this, you can try to grasp what another person's body language was saying about themselves. You can also take advantage of this innate and unconscious form of communication to improve the way you communicate in your marriage. By noticing your spouse's body language and altering your behavior accordingly, you can respond to their mood in a more sensitive fashion. You can also try to broadcast more open and intimate body language so that your partner feels more relaxed and engaged with you.

When good communication breaks down and messages aren't being correctly transferred between you and your spouse, it can lead to real issues in your marriage. There are several causes of miscommunication and misunderstanding. Failing to listen with full attention or using poorly chosen words are some of the biggest culprits of this. A real limitation of communication is that it depends on individual interpretation. In order to understand a message, we have to interpret it by comparing and contrasting it to things we already understand. This is essentially how the brain processes information — through association. This means that people can have very different interpretations of the same message, simply because they have different sets of associations in their mind that are triggered when they hear certain words or phrases. The connotations and inferred meaning of any one message can vary greatly from person to person. For example, one person may love dogs and positively receive communication from someone talking about dogs, a person with a fear of dogs may receive the exact same communication in a very different and much more negative manner. Your communication is therefore limited by yours and your audience's ability to process and understand what is being said. Accommodating for and overcoming these differences when it comes to your marriage involves speaking often and at length, to gain a better understanding of your spouse's communication style.

Chapter Two: Making Marriage Work

There are times in every marriage when it feels like things are hopeless. Being with someone in such a close and personal way for such a prolonged period while under pressure from yourselves and others is a perfect storm for conflict, issues, and difficulty to brew up at certain points throughout the course of your marriage. In this chapter, we'll be looking at what both you and your spouse have to do to make things work and get your marriage back on track and headed in the right direction.

Attitude, Mindset, and Perspective

As I indicated in the previous chapter, every marriage has roughly the same amount of unresolvable problems, whether it's a great marriage or a terrible one. What this tells us is that making your marriage not only work but be a beautiful and fulfilling experience for both you and your partner all comes down to the way the two of you perceive it and how you view each other. The attitude you have towards your marriage is the most important determining factor in the actual content and quality of the marriage itself.

The reason for this is that attitude and perspective shape everything in our lives. At the end of the day, things being good, bad, or somewhere between is simply a matter of how you choose to view things. Marriage is no different. Regardless of the actual objective quality of your marriage, the way you view it determines whether it is positive or negative. In fact, objectively. your marriage doesn't even exist, save for words on paper. It's a concept; it's subjective. What it is, is what you and your spouse view it as and therefore determine it to be.

This can be a difficult idea to wrap your head around at first, so stay with me here. I promise that if you can get to grips with this, everything else about your marriage will eventually fall into place. Your marriage is what it is; it could always be better, it could always be worse. No marriage or relationship is perfect. It's simply the nature of being human. If you decide to focus on the positive aspects of your marriage first, your marriage will seem a more positive thing in your mind. You will approach your spouse in a more upbeat and friendly way. You will be more grateful for all of the good things your marriage represents. Not that you should neglect the negative aspects of your marriage or ignore them completely — on the contrary, you should always seek to resolve issues wherever you can, learn from them, and then move on — but whether you focus on the positive or negative aspects of your relationship is a choice that you can and do make, every second of every day. Every thought you have or word you speak to your partner is either positive or negative in context. It either comes from a place of love or a place of hate. If you make the constant decision to try to view your marriage in a more positive light, in a more loving and grateful and appreciative way, it will become more positive over time. When both you and your spouse commit to trying to see the good in your marriage rather than dwelling on the bad, incredible things are possible. Attitude is the key to restarting your relationship, recalibrating your mind, and refocusing your attention on all of the beautiful things your marriage stands for.

In exactly the same way, it can alter your mindset towards conflict and issues in order for these unavoidable obstacles to appear in a more positive light. A marriage is about a bond between you and your spouse. The two of you are a team, even when it doesn't feel like it. You need to have each other's backs through thick and thin. It should be 'me and you versus the problem' rather than 'me versus you', every time. This first attitude promotes teamwork and working together to overcome obstacles as a unit. The latter does nothing but breed resentment. It doesn't matter who's to blame; we're all to blame for something, sooner or later. What's really important is being able to sit down and work out how to solve an issue rather than worrying about who's right and who's wrong.

Making a marriage work requires total commitment to the journey, no matter where it might take you. There will be difficulties, of course, but there always are in life. There's no way to avoid it; it's the way things are. Having a perfect, frictionless relationship or marriage isn't possible and should never be your goal. Instead, you should seek to be able to deal with issues in an emotionally healthy and productive way when they come up, rather than lapsing into shouting matches or blaming each other. Respect, honesty, trust, and effort are the cornerstones of any marriage, and making sure all four of these are present in both you and your spouse's minds is essential to making things work.

Often, marriages fall apart because things get stale. Once the honeymoon period has worn off and the flames of infatuation have died down a bit, people tend to feel like they have lost the passion somewhere along the way. They might feel less excited about their spouse or grow used to them being there and start to crave the tension and excitement of a new relationship. The beginning of a relationship is characterized by chemicals such as dopamine being released in both your brain and that of your partner. This is why relationships feel so exciting at first — there's a rush of chemicals in your brain that makes you feel incredible. Lots of people get hooked on this feeling, going from relationship to relationship to get their next hit of dopamine and ride the high of a new romance. Others make the mistake of equating this feeling with love. Once they've been with someone for a while, especially after marriage, the flames tend to die down and the chemicals that cause this feeling wear off and stop being released in such high doses; they feel like something's changed, like the love has worn off. This isn't the case, however. The love hasn't gone anywhere, because the feelings they felt before weren't love. It was just the rush from of bonding chemicals that come from a new relationship.

What is love, then, if not that feeling? That's a question that even philosophers have grappled with and struggled to answer. In my view, love is something far deeper than the shallow feelings caused by chemicals in your brain when you first start hooking up with someone new. Love is a choice; it's an attitude. It's the decision to treat your partner well because you care about them and want them to be happy. It's something much deeper and more fulfilling than any dopamine rush could ever be. It's the smoldering, glowing heat that's left once all the flames have died down — and it burns much, much hotter than any flame ever could. This is the reality of human romantic relationships. It doesn't matter who you're with, eventually, the flames of infatuation will subside, and you're left with something beautiful and enduring. This doesn't mean the passion has to leave your marriage, however. Things only get stale if you neglect the relationship and allow them to get stale. You can stoke the fire and add more fuel by putting in the effort to keep things fresh and spice it up. You never know all there is to know about a person, no matter how long you've been with them. If you keep up a desire to continuously learn about your spouse and remain excited to explore life together, you'll always feel close to them and passionate about being with them.

Expectations

An important part of getting your attitude and mindset right when it comes to your marriage is to have a healthy perspective on things by managing your expectations. Everyone has different preferences and different ideas about how things should be. People are independent and autonomous, and what appeals to one half of a married couple might not appeal to the other. This is not a bad thing, it's just another part of being human. Disappointment occurs when the reality of a situation fails to live up to the expectation we had of it beforehand. This can lead to a multitude of issues, both small and large, within the context of a long-term relationship or marriage.

A common result of mismanaged expectations is one partner feeling like they just aren't good enough for their spouse. They feel constantly criticized and critiqued, as though they're always being assessed and can't ever do enough to please their other half or meet their expectations. The result of this is that they always feel on edge and unable to relax around their partner for fear of doing something they judge to be 'wrong' or unacceptable. No relationship should feel this way; certainly not a marriage. Being married to someone should mean you're able to feel totally relaxed and at home when you're together, not like you're on parole.

The solution to a situation like this is two-fold. While constant criticism is abrasive and undermines a relationship because it forms a pattern of consistent negative behavior, it's often about relatively insignificant individual circumstances grouped together over a period of time. This makes it easy to overreact, particularly when it feels like it's never ending. A slight snide remark or sarcastic comment can be the straw that breaks the camel's back. With this in mind, whenever you find yourself on the receiving end of your partner's unrealistic expectations, take a deep breath and try to remain calm. Your fight-or-flight response has been triggered because of what you perceive to be a threat to your happiness, ego, or self-esteem. When this response is active, your prefrontal cortex — the part of your brain responsible for reasoning, evaluation, and rational thought — isn't able to function normally. This reduction in your ability to think logically can make you snap and overreact, causing the situation to rapidly spiral out of control.

Healthy communication about what each person expects from themselves, each other, and the marriage is necessary to set things straight and avoid future conflict. The best time to do this is early on in the relationship, and the second best time is right now. If you don't talk openly about what you need, want, and expect from your marriage, how is your spouse supposed to understand what they need to do in order for the both of you to be happy? Your job is to love each other and try your best to understand one another. When we understand each other better, we become less irritated by each other, and this is only possible through open and honest communication about our expectations.

Dealing With Bitterness And Resentment

These two things characterize every dysfunctional, unhappy marriage. The negative experiences we have with our spouses lead to us becoming jaded and withdrawn, holding grudges against each other and wishing that they would change. Conflict leads to defensiveness, reaction, overreaction and contempt on both sides. Communication becomes difficult, and communication about difficult issues becomes all but impossible. Under these circumstances, maintaining a healthy and fulfilling marriage seems like a pipe dream. We begin to stonewall one another, withdrawing emotionally from the relationship we have with our spouses and meeting any attempts at reconciliation with defensiveness and skepticism. When we grow to resent the people we love the most, it feels like there's too much bad blood to ever go back to the way things were. Too much has changed. Every interaction feels like it has a dark cloud hanging over it. We become so sick and tired of being hurt that we begin to expect it at every turn, so we become openly hostile to stop ourselves from having to experience the agony of being hurt any more.

The thing is, the current reality of our relationships and marriages are not decided by what has happened in the past, but by the attitude we bring to them now. If we decide to bring a negative attitude shaped by the bad experiences we've had before, our current reality will be negative, too. We always have a choice when we interact with someone else; we treat them in a way that stems from a place of love or a place of hate. If we're going to make things work with any one person, we have to choose to treat them with love, kindness, and compassion in the present moment, regardless of their actions in the past or present. Ask yourself, 'what kind of person do I want to be? What kind of marriage do I want to have?' The way you treat and think about your spouse shapes the quality of the relationship that you have with them. Making it work means making a commitment to leave bitterness and resentment behind and move on.

Positive, healthy communication based on the correct principles and coming from the right place is essential to moving past the difficulties we experience in marriage. You've loved each other enough to choose to get married, so you need to make a decision to treat each other with love and kindness now. Throughout my years as a therapist, I've heard countless married couples tell me that they hate and despise each other. And yet, in my experience, this isn't true the vast majority of the time, even if they think it is. It isn't possible to feel strong hate for something unless you blame it for causing the loss of something you love. Almost all of the couples who claimed to hate each other were simply grieving for the love they'd once had and lost and blamed each other for ruining. The love was still there underneath; it never went away. All they needed to do was to learn to see things from a different perspective. To put their egos aside, commit to making things work, and then work together to overcome their problems. Hate is always a reaction to hurt. When we're hurting, we lash out and we hurt the people we love, who in turn hurt and hate us out of the hurt they're experiencing. This is just another unfortunate aspect of the human condition. When we feel threatened or cornered, such as when we're forced into a difficult conversation we're not ready to have, we lash out. Sometimes people lash out and there's no apparent cause — whatever it is, it's hidden. Their behavior is simply a manifestation of whatever has caused them hurt, whether it's something you've done or something totally unrelated to the relationship that you have with them.

When you decide to choose love, to put the bitterness and resentment aside and focus on reconnecting emotionally with your partner, your relationship will change before your very eyes. You'll find you become more observant and grateful for the good things about your spouse and your marriage. There's power in gratitude; being grateful for things changes your outlook and perspective on your relationship. If you communicate this gratitude to your spouse, your relationship will begin to thaw, no matter how frosty things might be. Choosing love is about communicating the value you place on your relationship and on your spouse to them. Appreciate your spouse and tell them why. You can do this in any number of sweet and thoughtful ways that allow you to demonstrate what they mean to you. You can leave sweet messages for them on the refrigerator or in their lunch, or come home early from work just to spend time with them. Let them know that your life is better because they're in it.

Change the energy of your relationship in order to influence the perception that you and your partner have of it and of each other. Avoid criticism wherever you can, particularly if it's over something trivial, and where you can't avoid it, be kind, compassionate, loving, and tactful in your criticism. Bear in mind that criticism doesn't have to be intended or even real in order to have negative effects on your marriage — it only has to be perceived. Try to change the way you interact with your partner to come from a place of love, rather than a place of indifference or negativity and hate. Change your mindset towards your marriage, and most importantly change the way you deal with problems. Remember, it's the two of you against the problem, every time, regardless of what the problem is. Respect each other as allies and friends as well as partners. Focus on being positive and bringing positivity into your marriage, no matter how much of an uphill battle that might appear to be at first. The hardest part of these things is always getting started. Act and speak as often as you can from a place of compassion, kindness, patience, and understanding. Love is an effort, and you have to put in as much of it as you can to put the resentment behind you.

Most importantly, you have to be able to forgive. Forgiveness is no easy feat. It will take all the patience and understanding you're able to muster. It might help to remember that things rarely turn out the way we want or plan them to. Things simply unfold, and we sometimes find ourselves in situations where there's no easy way out. You're in this together, and no matter what might have happened in the past, if both of you regret any wrongdoing and mistakes and want to push on together towards a better future, it doesn't matter. I've had many clients over the years who believed that their marriage was on life support and well past making a healthy recovery. Too much had happened; there were too many bad feelings, too many lies, too much infidelity, and resentment and ill-feeling. In almost every case, their marriage wasn't past repair, no matter how badly damaged it might have been. As I've said before, the circumstances don't matter. I've seen it all. The only thing that really matters when it comes to marriage, in the end, is the willingness to try to make things work. That alone can overcome any number of problems.

What Destroys A Marriage?

Everybody has different ideas about what causes divorce. Every divorce results from its own unique story of hurt and misery. The one thing that rings true through virtually every destroyed marriage I've experienced in my career is that ultimately, most of the pain we feel isn't caused by other people but comes from within ourselves. It's not out there, it's not caused by the people or the circumstances in your life; ultimately, it's inside you. Most people fail to realize this and stay married and miserable because of it. They blame others for their problems but deep down they know that they'd be unhappy no matter who they were with.

You can stay married, but you don't have to stay miserable. Leaving someone or getting a divorce is no guarantee of happiness, anyway. It won't take away the pain or emptiness that's inside us. Our subconscious minds rule us. We're programmed to act in the way we act. This is something we don't like to admit to ourselves. Everyone likes to believe that they're acting of their own free will. The truth is, we're wired to be the way we are by our genetics and the way we've been shaped by the things that happened to us in life, particularly in childhood. We tend to treat our husbands and wives the way we witnessed our parents treating each other while we were growing up. The things we're exposed to as children serve as templates on which we model our behavior as adults without even realizing it. This process is known as 'imprinting'. It shapes everything about our future selves, from our loyalties and standards to our behavior. Some people are programmed by this process to be 'leavers,' while others are programmed to want to stay. We're programmed to meet conflict by either shutting down or flaring up with anger. Patterns that are formed in childhood can, therefore, end up destroying marriages as adults.

This is particularly true for those of us who were victims of physical or emotional abuse in our childhood. Abuse, neglect, and abandonment all leave deep and lasting scars, terrible pain inside that we struggle to process. This then affects our marriages later in life when the programming is triggered and resurfaces. We then find ourselves caught in a tornado of pain and misery that sweeps away all of the people and things that we love and that are important to us. Becoming aware of our programming and talking about our childhood experiences with our spouse helps us to deal with the pain inside and overcome our childhood programming. Communication is the key, not pushing the one we love away from us out of pain and fear. Most marriages are destroyed from the inside out, not from the outside in. Fortifying the bond you have with your spouse through positive and open communication about difficult emotional issues can help the two of you to help each other through difficult times and stay together.

Improving Your Marriage

When it comes to improving the quality of your marriage, you first need to embrace a paradox of sorts. The truth is that you don't really need to improve it as such; you just need to change how you perceive it. If you change the way you see your marriage, you'll make it a more positive thing to be a part of. The first step in making it better is to acknowledge that it's already good. If you scoff at this and believe your marriage is truly bad, I urge you to think again. The fact that you're reading or listening to this book in the first place suggests that you really want to try to save your marriage, so there must be something there worth saving. Even if you think your marriage is a negative thing overall, there will always be positive and redeeming aspects of it. Focus on these parts of your relationship with your spouse rather than the negative things.

Simply put, your marriage is what it is — it can always be better, and it can always be worse. You're wired to judge and evaluate everything in your life, so try to judge your relationship in a certain way. Rather than always telling each other and yourself how bad things are, try instead to think and talk about how good it is. Your reality is whatever you pay attention to, so pay attention to all the good things about your spouse. Document the ways your marriage is a great thing to be a part of and appreciate and enjoy them. Show your spouse what they mean to you, and your marriage will begin to improve.

Developing an Action Plan to Make Your Marriage Work

An effective way of implementing real, lasting change in your marriage is to develop an action plan. This is a structured, formulaic way of approaching your marriage, meaning you can both agree upon it and then go ahead and work on it together while charting your progress. One of the best ways I've found to put this method into action is to sit down together and draw up a list of all the steps you want to take as a couple to get your marriage back and track and make progress together. These should be tailored to your specific situation and can be anything that the two of you need to do to make things work, as long as you can both do them together.

The first thing you need to do is make a list of all the areas of conflict and disagreement in your marriage. From this, you can then work out what you need to do to make your action plan work for your marriage. I'd also recommend considering the following 12 steps when drawing up your plan:

1. **Focus on yourself:** You can't control the actions of anyone other than yourself — not even your spouse. All you can do is

work on yourself and hold up your half of the action plan. If your spouse is struggling, then you should be there to support them, but you can't work on them or change them from the outside. Lasting change always comes from within.

2. **Learn to express concerns positively:** This is also known as constructive criticism. Part of being a good spouse and a good friend to someone is to be there to tell them the uncomfortable truths that they might not want to hear. While it's your job to express your concerns, you don't have to be spiteful about it. Think about how you can phrase things to your spouse when you're bringing up an issue to give them a more positive, supportive, constructive spin on the problem. This will help them deal with the issues they're facing in a much

healthier way, rather than feeling like you're just being overly critical and petty.

3. **Commit to making decisions together:** When you're married, the two of you are a team. The things you do affect each other in a very personal and direct way. As such, it's only right that you should make big decisions together, because your spouse deserves to have a say in decisions that will affect them as well as you. Additionally, consider that your spouse should represent the most intimate and well-developed relationship you have in your life. A healthy marriage is one where each person seeks each other's advice and counsel because they respect one another's opinions.

4. **Work on your energy:** Through your actions, words, and attitude, you bring a

certain energy and intensity to your marriage. You can control and shape this energy to focus it in different areas and into different moods. You can and should work to improve the type and amount of energy you bring to your marriage to try to make it as positive as possible. While it's not healthy to fake how you feel or pretend that you're fine when you're not just for the sake of your spouse, you can influence how you feel by paying attention to the right things. You should try your best to keep your energy positive by focusing on the good things in your life and marriage, rather than paying attention to all of the negative aspects of your life.

5. **Speak openly and often:** Communicate, communicate, communicate. You need to talk to your

spouse frequently, and the quality of the communication needs to be as high as possible. While you don't have to be glued at the hip to your spouse, find and take all opportunities to talk that you can. Remember to try to listen more than you speak, and when you speak, speak from the heart. Be open about how you feel and what you think. Try to stick to your word by meaning what you say; this is known as having integrity and will make your marriage a thousand times better.

6. **Trust each other:** Trust is the bedrock that relationships are built on. Without it, being married is like trying to construct a cathedral on foundations made of sand; it just can't be done. The whole thing implodes and sinks in on itself before long. Trust has to be earned, it's true, but trust also has to be given to make things

work. You have to accept the fact that some people will hurt you in life, and that all you can do is trust the ones you love; the rest is up to them. Some would go even further and say that everybody hurts you eventually. Part of learning to love your life is working out who is worth hurting for. If there are serious reasons for a deep lack of trust in your relationship, we'll be going over how to work on rebuilding it in the fourth chapter of this book, no matter how bad it gets — so hang in there.

7. **Show gratitude and appreciation:** There are few things more exhausting than working hard and trying your best only to feel underappreciated and unacknowledged for your effort. Cultivating a happier, healthier marriage is only possible if you're able to recognize

your spouse's loving actions and support by sincerely thanking them and telling them that you appreciate them for everything they do.

8. **Show emotion:** No matter how foreign it might feel to wear your heart on your sleeve and put your emotions on show, it's an important part of being human and being in a loving relationship. You're not a rock. Your someone's husband or wife. You're a human being, and you feel emotion. That's a beautiful thing. Without emotion, life would be meaningless. Embrace the full spectrum of your life and show and tell your spouse how you feel. When you're excited, when you're happy, when you're sad: it doesn't matter. Be yourself, be open, and show them how you really feel inside rather than keeping those feelings to yourself.

9. **Be honest:** Total honesty can be a very bitter and difficult pill to swallow, but if you genuinely want to forge a marriage that lasts and is full of loving and happy memories when you look back on it at the end of your life, it's essential. You absolutely have to be honest with your spouse, no matter how hard it is. You have to have the humility to hold your hands up and admit when you're wrong. You have to be grounded enough to admit your mistakes and seek forgiveness. Nothing else will do. Without honesty, a marriage can never go the distance. No matter how good you might be at keeping things to yourself, something will slip eventually. Your spouse will find out what it is that you don't want them to know, and it will break the trust in your relationship. If you really want to make things work, then work on being honest.

10. **Support and respect:** Your job as a spouse and a partner is to be there for your other half through thick and thin. You need to be their rock when times are hard and they need to return the favor for you when it's your turn to need a shoulder to cry on. You support, uplift, and encourage each other not from a sense of duty but from mutual respect that transcends everything else. You love each other. You're on the same team: your team. No one else comes close; it's the two of you. So be there for each other, and never sell each other out. If you can't rely on your spouse to have your back when the chips are down, then who can you rely on?

11. **Touch often:** True intimacy and genuine emotional closeness aren't possible without physical contact. Once this

dwindles in a marriage, people begin to pull away from each other. Physical distance mirrors emotional distance. Increasing one will increase the other, and the reverse is also true. When you're not touching each other in a loving and affectionate way on a regular basis, you will begin to grow apart. You have to reintroduce frequent and extended periods of physical contact to reconnect with your spouse and improve your marriage. Small things like holding hands and cuddling are just as important as having sex and kissing each other on the cheek.

12. **Make the effort:** No relationship can last when one or both halves of the couple aren't putting in the effort, and marriage is no different. Just because you're legally bound to one another doesn't mean that

you can just kick back and relax your standards without the bond you have suffering. Work hard to make your spouse feel special and loved. Have fun with each other. Don't let the passion wilt. Go out on dates. Be spontaneous. Do things you've never done before and do them together. Life is short and you're with each other because you love each other. Embrace life with your best friend. Have fun.

Chapter Three:
Dealing With Porn Addiction

This topic is such a common issue now in the information age with everyone having access to the internet, I've dedicated a whole chapter to it. Porn addiction is a particularly tricky subject to deal with, both because the intimate and private nature of masturbation means it can be embarrassing and difficult to talk about and because many people suffering from it struggle to admit that they have a problem, even to themselves.

Porn and the Brain

In order to address how to deal with a porn addiction, we first have to look at the background surrounding what porn does to a person's brain and why it can be so damaging and so difficult to deal with. Contrary to popular belief, both men and women can suffer from an addiction to porn, although it's true that men tend to be more prone and vulnerable to it. This is because of the biological differences in how men and women perceive and react to sex and sexual stimuli. By and large, men are attracted to and focus on the physical aspects of women. This results from evolutionary biology; we're programmed to want to reproduce (or, at least, to do the things that fulfill our drive and cause us to reproduce). It's in our DNA, coded into us over millions and millions of years of evolution. However, there are stark biological differences in the way that men and women reproduce that influence our behavior when it comes to sex.

First, men have no way to guarantee that offspring is theirs (in an evolutionary context, disregarding modern science, of course). This is in contrast to women, who have to grow, carry, and give birth to a baby. They have total parental certainty; they have successfully passed their genes on. The result of this is that in order for men to make sure that they have passed on their genes, they have to rely on putting their eggs in as many baskets as possible, so to speak. They're genetically coded to want to diversify, to spread their sperm around in order to toy ensure that at least some women carry their children for them. This means that they're naturally prone to want to sleep with as many women as possible. They're attracted to all of the things that signal to them that a woman is fertile, healthy, and likely able to bear their children; such as wide 'child-bearing' hips. This makes porn particularly appealing to men. The dominantly visual aspect of it presses all of their evolutionary buttons. The same isn't necessarily true for women. Since they don't have to worry about the uncertainty of passing on their genes, they tend to instead seek men who will provide the resources they need to look after their child and make sure of their reproductive success by helping their offspring to survive and reach adulthood. Women tend to, therefore, be more attracted to things that indicate a suitable partner; such as personality, intelligence, and the ability to provide resources. Women tend to be less attracted to men's bodies and more attracted to the role that a man can play for them; sex is therefore usually a more emotional attraction for women.

Setting this aside for a minute, we now must look at what porn does to our brains. In order to do this, we have to think about the context of modern technology and how it can present us with very different circumstances than we've evolved to experience. Men are programmed to seek variety and novelty in order to maximize their chances of reproductive success. With online pornography, they can see more women in a sexual context in a short period of browsing than their ancestors would have been lucky to see in a lifetime. Men's brains tend to be more prone to being hijacked by porn because it temporarily satisfies a very primal and unscratchable itch. Porn can totally carry away the pleasure center of their brains with nearly limitless fulfillment and will cause a person to seek to indulge in it as often as they can.

Part of the reason porn is so addictive relates to the biological, chemical nature of our brains. Porn and masturbation stimulate dopamine release. We get addicted to the chemical kick that results from doing these things. This kick is a very short but intense one, not unlike incredibly addictive drugs like crack cocaine. This can make people constantly crave it or have it on their mind at all times, with an urge so overwhelmingly powerful it turns into a compulsion many people find themselves powerless to resist. This can have serious consequences for a person's sex life, particularly if they're married. Porn offers a very direct, convenient, visually satisfying, novelty-indulging, erotic stimuli that sex in the real world just can't live up to. This can affect a marriage or relationship due to the differences in expectation over the sex life of the couple. For example, a wife may feel neglected and overlooked because her husband gets all of his kicks from porn instead of having sex with her. To the porn user, sex just isn't as fulfilling or gratifying as their addiction, and so it wins every time.

Another aspect of porn addiction that needs to be addressed is that a person can become desensitized to sex in a number of ways. First of all, the novelty, variety, and convenience they've come to crave and expect to be sexually fulfilled just isn't there. Secondly, because they've become accustomed to a certain amount, type, and frequency of stimulation from masturbation, some people, especially men, can find it very hard to climax from sex alone. Neither of these side effects are particularly conducive to a mutually fulfilling sex life for a married couple.

Overcoming Porn Addiction

In order to overcome a porn addiction, it's important for a sufferer to first understand the operating equipment of their own mind. They can use this knowledge to deconstruct the process that is happening in their mind when they feel the urge to watch porn. The first thing that needs to be kept in mind is the nature of the problem: a person with a porn addiction isn't the problem. They aren't somehow a more flawed or a worse person than anyone else. Any addiction or compulsion is perpetuated by itself; the more it is indulged, the more entrenched it becomes and the harder it is to kick. Every time a person watches porn and masturbates to get the reward, the more conditioned they become to associate porn with sexual satisfaction. A chemical reaction is triggered, and they become addicted to the chemical rush in their brain. This makes it very difficult to deprogram themselves from the addiction; their brain is telling them to look after themselves because they have a need that can be taken care of. The only way to really overcome it is to break the vicious cycle of reinforcement that is sustained by indulging addictive, compulsive behavior such as watching porn and masturbating. Breaking this cycle can only be done through abstaining from the desire to watch porn.

Obviously, this is more easily said than done. Overcoming addiction involves rewiring your brain on a chemical and cognitive level. Luckily, because of the neuroplasticity of our grey matter, we can do this by changing our behavior. Porn is a purely psychological dependence, so when the behavior is changed, the dependence can be broken relatively simply, if not easily. Real and lasting changes in behavior have to come from within, from a person's desire to better themselves and have greater control over their biological urges, and from the willpower to wield a greater amount of influence over their own day-to-day lives. As is the case with trying to overcome any addictive behavior, relapse is inevitable. If accepting you have a problem is the first step to overcoming it, then accepting that you will relapse at some point and adopting an attitude of forgiveness towards yourself for it is the second.

Whenever we're faced with an addictive craving, we have to remember that we always have a choice as to how we act, even when it feels like we don't. We make the decision to indulge a behavior, rather than just failing to resist it. This is the harsh truth of any psychological addiction or dependency. However, when our brains are wired a certain way and we expect ourselves to indulge it, we often fall victim to it no matter how strong our willpower is. Despite this, you might find it helpful to mentally press the pause button when you feel the urge to watch porn and remember that you are going to decide what it is that you're about to do. Whether you make a positive or negative choice is up to you. You always have the opportunity to say no, to not indulge the behavior.

Distraction is a fundamental part of overcoming a porn addiction. When you feel the urge to watch it, resisting while remaining still mentally and physically turns it into a sheer battle of willpower. There's also something of a catch-22 involved here because the harder you try not to think of something, the harder it gets to not think about it. If you instead purposefully distract yourself, the craving will soon be forgotten and the urge to consume porn will subside. Some of the best forms of distraction are ones that involve doing something active mentally or physically in order to occupy your mind and body and take your thoughts away from porn. You could exercise by working out or going for a run or a walk, read a book, or even sit and quietly meditate by focusing on your breathing in order to calm your mind. Your end goal is simply to break the grip that pornography has over you by avoiding watching it or masturbating to it when you feel like you want to. If you can exert restraint and self-control over your actions on a regular basis and not give in to it, it's power over you will begin to slip and you will be able to reclaim control over your sex life. Porn is extremely powerful stuff, so it has to be used responsibly in order to avoid it becoming a serious problem in your life and marriage.

If your spouse is the one with the addiction to porn, then your job is to encourage and support them while trying your very best to be as understanding and non-invasive as possible. You need to understand that this situation is highly personal, and trying too hard to control your spouse's porn habits (and therefore sex life) will only lead to defensiveness on their part and more hostility between the two of you. Your role, just as much as the sufferer, is to understand the nature of the problem. Porn use tends to have moral implications for a lot of people, particularly religious folk, but it doesn't have anything to do with the quality of a person's character or their commitment to their marriage or family. The person isn't the problem; their brain chemistry is, and they can't help the way they're wired and that the internet and the porn industry exploits this. Instead of freaking out and overreacting and making out like it's the worst thing in the world, instead try to get some perspective.

Quick tip: Put yourself in your spouse's shoes and try to help them through empathy, rather than judging them. Don't make more or less of it than it is. It is what it is. Lots of people watch porn, and lots of people get addicted to it. How we perceive and respond to our addictions triggers our reaction to it. It can be easy for a person having their porn habits questioned to feel threatened and shut down completely, so try your best to be as sensitive as possible. The wrong approach may make the problem worse, particularly if you trigger your spouse's fight-or-flight response. Be loving, be forgiving, and be accepting. Remember to try and tackle the problem as a team, but remember that you can't control what anyone other than yourself does. This is something your partner ultimately has to do alone, so just try to be there for them and provide a judgment-free forum for them to express themselves to you.

Chapter Four: Rebuilding Broken Trust

As I've mentioned previously, trust is the foundation of any relationship. Once trust has been lost in a marriage, there's no going back to the way things were before. In this chapter, we'll examine why trust is so important, how it's broken, and how to rebuild it and your marriage after it's gone.

The Nature of Trust

Trust is a very strange concept, but it's one we're all intimately familiar with. It all stems from the nature of ourselves as human beings. We're vulnerable, finite creatures. We can be harmed, or taken advantage of, so we're safest when we have friends and allies; when we're in a group. We're highly social and tribal by nature, prone to surrounding ourselves with friends and family who all help to support each other so that we benefit mutually and have a better chance of survival. This emphasis on teamwork and cooperation means that we have to trust the people we're close with. If we don't trust, we can't let them be a true part of our lives, but when we trust, we give others the power to hurt us in some way.

Nowhere does this context of trust carry more weight than in a marriage. When we're married to someone, we're meant to be closer to them than to any other person we know. They are supposed to be our best friend and life partner, someone who always has our back, someone we can always rely on. They have the power to lift us up to heights that we didn't realise existed or tear us down. We give them the key to our hearts, and we have to trust that they mean what they say, that they love us as much as we love them and that they won't hurt us.

True trust has to be earned; it can't just be given away freely. It would take someone very naive to completely trust a stranger they'd just met. We have to demonstrate to others that we're good, trustworthy people if they're going to trust us at all. I like to think of trust like a savings account you might have with a bank. We have one of these accounts with each person we know, and everyone we know has one with us. When we do something that shows a person they can trust us, we make a deposit into this balance. If it's a small gesture, it might only be a small deposit. When we really help someone out or come to their aid in a time of need, especially without direct benefit to ourselves, these deposits can be much larger. Over time, these accounts grows considerably, with people we know well carrying a very high trust balance with us. When something happens that undermines that trust in some way, a withdrawal is made and the balance decreases; whether this is a large withdrawal or a small one depends on the context of the trust being undermined.

Infidelity and Lies

Every relationship and marriage will experience small withdrawals of trust sometimes. Everybody makes mistakes and handles situations badly, but most of the time these withdrawals are small and insignificant enough that once the problem is dealt with and motivations are explained, we deposit the withdrawn amount once more, perhaps even with a bit of interest. However, there are some things that can cause the trust in a marriage to be completely shattered, with virtually the entire balance withdrawn in one go. The two most common causes of trust being eroded quickly tend to go hand in hand with each other: infidelity and lies.

While not all lying in a marriage results from infidelity, virtually all instances of infidelity are followed by lies. Whether this means someone telling outright falsities to cover their tracks or simply lying by omission. Married couples will lie to each other about all kinds of things, however, and it always has negative consequences for their marriage one way or another. With the exception of innocent white lies, lying in any relationship slowly and insidiously erodes the trust that lies at the heart of it. Regardless of whether or not lies are exposed and revealed, they always have a corrosive and harmful effect on the relationship. When they are exposed, and a person realizes that their spouse has been lying to them, it brings up a whole host of other issues. If they were capable of lying about A, then who knows if they've been telling the truth about B through Z? Once the lying starts, it opens a can of worms. Unless the motivations for lying are explained, apologized, and taken responsibility for, it can lead to a slippery slope where the lied to partner doesn't know where to draw the line and continue to trust their spouse. When the lying goes unnoticed, it's only a matter of time. A lie that passes the first test and seems to go undetected is like an unexploded mine. It's only a matter of time before it's stepped on and blows up.

We tend to only lie to our spouses when we have something to hide and because we think that we have something to lose by telling the truth. This means that once a lie has been told about something significant, we have to lie again and again in order to cover our tracks and keep the original lie concealed. We have to maintain an awareness of what is a lie and what is truth to avoid our lying being discovered, which is an exhausting, draining exercise. As pathological liars know only too well, there comes a point after enough lying where you can no longer discern fact from fiction and lies simply become a part of what you come to think of as the truth. After all of this effort, a single slip and the whole story can come unraveled in one go, leaving the trust shattered and requiring a lot of communication and honesty to rebuild.

Nothing can break the trust in a marriage quite like infidelity and the lying that usually comes with it. Being faithful is a huge part of any monogamous relationship, and straying from your partner to hook up with someone else on the side can end even the strongest of marriages in one clean stroke. This is why so many of us try to cover up our mistakes when we've been unfaithful, although more lying only makes the problem worse when the very best thing to do is come clean. When a marriage has had problems with lying and/or infidelity, the trust has been broken, and the balance is withdrawn, it is possible to rebuild and save the marriage. It takes time, patience, forgiveness, and a lot of understanding, but it can be done.

Rebuilding Trust

The first thing that has to be understood about rebuilding trust is that when the trust in any relationship is seriously violated, there's no way to go back to how things were before. The dynamic has been changed for good. The old relationship is dead and gone; you have to start again from scratch. If the two of you can make things work, it will be in a new relationship, like a phoenix rising from the ashes of the old. Learning to trust someone again after they've let you down badly is a long and difficult journey. You might never be able to trust them again.

Whether or not it's possible to rebuild the trust in your marriage once it has been broken is a matter of context and your own values. What constitutes a dealbreaker to some people is more of a gray area for others. Some people see infidelity as the ultimate death knell or the final nail in the coffin, and won't let themselves remain married to someone who could betray them so badly, whereas others will do just about anything to make things work and stay together. My professional two cents on the matter is that context and circumstance are everything. If your spouse cheated on you once in a drunken mistake, owned up to it immediately, is ashamed of themselves for letting you down, and is dedicated to making things right, that's one thing. It's very saveable. If, however, your spouse has been involved in a pattern of cheating and lying, and shows no intention of owning up to what they've done or committing to becoming a better person and partner to you, then a very persuasive argument can be made that you'd be better off divorcing them and leaving them in the past. Keep in mind that these are two extremes; most instances of trust being badly broken aren't nearly as black and white, and contain varying amounts of lying and obstructing and dodging the truth. At the end of the day, only you are in a position to decide whether it's best to end your marriage for good or commit to trying to make it work.

Rebuilding Trust as the Perpetrator

Hurting the people we love is just another unfortunate aspect of being human. All too often, we hurt others because we're hurting ourselves, and we don't know how to deal with that pain in a way that is healthy. So we lash out, get ourselves into difficult situations, and end up bitterly regretting our actions when we realize what we've done. If you're the reason the trust has been broken in your marriage and you want to know what you need to do to get that back and reestablish a healthy relationship with your spouse, the first thing you need to do is forgive yourself — no matter how badly you want to hate and punish yourself.

Forgiveness is the path of healing that we can all choose to take at any time. Your spouse will have to forgive you in time, but that's not the most important thing right now. For them to forgive you and come to trust and respect you again, you have to first communicate openly and at length about what happened and why. This can't happen until you've begun the process of healing, and the first step on that long road is to forgive and understand yourself. Everybody makes mistakes. No one is perfect. True self-love comes from feeling ashamed, or guilty, or angry, or scared, and not resenting yourself for feeling that way.

Then you have to engage in a period of open conversation with your spouse about what has happened and why the trust between the two of you has been broken. You need to be completely honest with them, and they with you. The two of you need to work as a team to look at and address all the reasons your marriage got to this state in the first place, and how you're going to work on them going forward. It's not enough to simply commit to working on the symptoms. You have to reach the underlying causes and understand exactly what the flaws of your marriage are to put them right and carry out lasting change. Remember that trust has to be earned, not given freely, and that this is especially the case when that trust has already been broken. In fact, once you've broken someone's trust so fundamentally, they have every right to never believe a word you say ever again. 'Once bitten, twice shy' — you will need to demonstrate that you can be trusted and that you're committed to changing and to your marriage over and over again to help your spouse trust you even a little after everything that's happened. In all likelihood, you broke their heart. You must make deposits and avoid withdrawals over an extended period of time to really convince them that they can once again give you the power to break their heart.

In order to show your spouse that they can trust you again and that whatever happened was a mistake that won't ever be repeated, it's important that you are completely open and honest with them. You need to lay it all out on the table, no matter how difficult that might be, or how many more issues doing so might bring up. You owe it to them and to yourself to tell the full truth, no matter how painful it is. It goes without saying that if you've been involved in an affair, you need to end it. The best time was right before it started; the second best time is right now. Not only should you end the affair, but if you're committed to making your marriage work you should totally cut ties with the person you've been unfaithful with. That means deleting their number and erasing all traces of them from your life, including from your social media. Lots of people feel squeamish about doing this, particularly because they're worried about coming across as rude. Don't even factor being polite into doing what you need to do to stay with your spouse. This isn't the time to be concerned about being rude. It's time to save your marriage. So do what you need to do and trust that the other person will find their own way in life. You must expect and accept a period of total transparency; if your spouse requests to check your phone and social media, you'll either have to accept that this is the price of breaking and trying to rebuild trust or refuse and be kicked to the curb for having something to hide. Marriage is a highly intimate experience; we have to share sacred parts of ourselves with our partner. Losing an element of privacy is often the price you have to pay for breaking your spouse's trust. It's also important to say what you're going to do and then do what you say. You need integrity now more than ever if you're going to do what you can to help your spouse trust you again. The rest is up to them.

Rebuilding Trust as the Victim

When you've had the horrible experience of being on the receiving end of a trust-shattering blow to your marriage, it's tempting to pack up and call it a day then and there. No one would hold it against you if you decided that was what was for the best. However, all is not lost. There is still hope for your marriage. You can still be happy and fulfilled with the person you married. You can rebuild the trust you've lost and turn things around. It doesn't have to be over unless you decide it's over. If you're both willing to make it work, then there's no obstacle that you can't adapt to and overcome.

Once you've made the decision to work past a major breach of trust, there's a lot of difficult work ahead that you'll have to dive into and begin to work through. It will be a very tough process, but with perseverance, you will get there. I've seen all kinds of married couples in all kinds of horrible situations pull through and overcome the odds because, at the end of the day, attitude is the most important thing. You're not the first people to face the issues you're facing as a couple, and you won't be the first to overcome them. Couples have faced much, much worse and come out the other side stronger and better for it. I can assure you of that — I've witnessed it myself. If both you and your spouse are dedicated and committed to making things work, then the circumstances of the past don't matter, and they won't decide whether or not you end up being able to break new ground together. The only deciding factor is whether or not the two of you really want to make things work together.

The first thing you need to know when it comes to rebuilding trust is that the lack of trust isn't the primary problem your marriage faces, but rather a secondary problem. The primary problem is whatever broke that trust in the first place, and the fact that broken trust results from one of the principles of your relationship being violated. Trust issues result from something that has already happened that damaged that trust, and this is where you should focus your attention first, rather than on the matter of trust itself. The trust will return as a result of ensuring that you and your spouse are both clear on and dedicated to following the core principles of your relationship and your marriage.

Any relationship is based on certain principles that form the core of the bond between two people. What these principles are and how they're approached characterize every relationship, from great, loving, healthy, lasting marriages to abusive nightmares. Principles are also important in the wider context of your life, as the principles you stick to determine your life's outcomes. If you're going to rebuild the trust you've lost and learn how to make things work, then you need to work on how the two of you perceive and process the principles of your relationship. Before you do this, however, it's essential to understand the importance of positivity. The attitude with which you approach the whole task of rebuilding trust and mending your marriage will determine how successful you are in ultimately achieving this. If you try to maintain a positive outlook and an optimistic state of mind, you'll very likely be successful. If however, you focus on the negatives and don't truly believe that things can actually change for the better between you and your spouse, then you'll be trapped in a situation of your own making and that will be your reality. Your mindset matters. How you think will determine your outcomes.

Once you've adopted the right attitude, you need to examine the principles and values of your marriage. These are the 'why' behind your entire relationship with your spouse; the shared sense of purpose you both possess. Many people won't examine these at all throughout the course of their marriage. Sometimes people end up forgetting why they're even together in the first place. Naturally, these vary from marriage to marriage, so you'll have to look at those things that make yours unique and work out where you both stand on them. Some of the most important ones in any relationship are:

1. **Humility:** This is when you don't put your own wants and needs above those of other people because you have a humble view of your own importance and realize that you're no better than anyone else just because you're you. It represents openness and a willingness to change, and is essential to making any marriage work. Too often, we believe that we are 100% right, and as a result we treat each other horribly. It's important to be able to put your own ego aside and acknowledge that who is right or wrong isn't important; working together is.

2. **Forgiveness:** This is the ability to leave the past in the past, to give up any demands that what has happened before

be any different to how it has played out now, and move on from hurt and resentment. At the end of the day, stuff happens in life. Everybody makes mistakes. If we aren't able to forgive, we live our whole lives miserable and holding grudges against the people we think have wronged us, as well as against ourselves.

3. **Respect** - Being a respectful person is an integral part of remaining happily married and making your marriage a success. It isn't just about treating your spouse respectfully, though. How you treat those around you and the people you interact with on a day-to-day basis — especially the people who can't do anything for you — says a lot about who you are as a person. Respect isn't just about respecting those that respect you, or respecting people only when they treat you with

respect. The true measure of a person's character is if they can be respectful towards everyone, regardless of whether or not that respect is reciprocated.

4. **Love:** This may seem like an obvious inclusion, but many people seem to assume that love is something that just comes naturally, as though it's simply a force of nature. This may be at least partly true, but in order to really love you have to make choices. Being married presents you with many different opportunities to make choices and decisions. You can always choose to love, and you have to make the decision to love your spouse every day of your life, no matter what. The two of you have to choose to love each other, to stick by each other even when times get tough and things get hard.

5. **Compassion and kindness:** Being married means you are someone's best friend and life partner. You should try your hardest to cultivate all of the love and compassion you possibly can for yourself and for your spouse, for both of your sakes. These two things go hand in hand and are like an infinite spring inside of you. The more you embrace these values and make them a part of your life and your marriage, the more you will feel their effects on your own mindstate and life. The more kindness and compassion you treat your spouse with, the more you will receive from them in turn.

6. **Work:** When it's all said and done, marriages require hard work — lots of it. The default trajectory of any relationship left to its own devices is down. In order to elevate the trajectory of your marriage and

keep on moving onwards and upwards, you need to put in the effort. You need to try, and you need to want to succeed at the endeavor of being married.

If you and your spouse apply the right principles to your marriage and commit to working through problems together, you can rebuild any broken trust with time. Although it may be difficult to believe in the aftermath of a significant breach of trust, with enough hard work you can come out on the other side of it with a stronger marriage and a better understanding of each other than you had before the trust was lost. You can be happier, healthier, and more satisfied together than you ever imagined was possible by sticking together and pulling through when the chips are down. You can use the broken trust as the catalyst that propels your marriage to new heights, to heal and strengthen it and prevent such occurrences from ever happening again.

A point that I think is worth making here is that no matter how tempting it might seem, you should not seek revenge on your spouse for anything they've done to you. I've had many clients over the years who expressed a desire to 'even the score' with their spouse, particularly in cases of infidelity. Most people don't follow through with these urges, but those who do inevitably regret it. In order for true healing and forgiveness to take place, the slate needs to be wiped clean. The past is the past. What's done is done. Your spouse can't take any of it back, although they might wish they could. If you're going to have any chance of making things work between the two of you, then you have to leave the infidelity, the lying, the resentment, and the petty desires for revenge in the past. Adding to that will only end up making the problem worse and muddying what might be the only chance you have of rebuilding the trust that is so vital to your marriage. Don't throw it all away just to get even — you'll only end up regretting it.

Perhaps the very best thing you can do to heal the wounds you have from having your trust broken is to talk about it. Express yourself. Share what happened with the people around you, the people you trust. Talk to your friends and family, or a therapist if you need someone impartial and professional. Talking about things helps us to work out what we think and how we feel about the things that happen to us. It helps us to get our heads around the problems we face and makes us feel more in control of the situation. However, there is something that you should try to keep in mind when it comes to talking to people about what has happened to you. When we're hurt and offended, we tend to create a story that we tell people in order to explain what has happened. While this is natural and beneficial in helping you to recover, take care not to make yourself out to be the victim. Even if you are totally blameless and the victim of circumstance and other people, it stops you from letting go. When we feel like the victim, we feel resentful and hard done by. This can stop you from being able to move on from the things that have happened because you're too hung up on being the helpless victim to allow yourself to let it go.

Quick tip: You should also make the time to communicate openly with your spouse. Not just about the breach of trust — although you will likely feel the need to talk to them at length and often about that - but also in terms of just enjoying each other's company. For healing to take place, you need to learn to view them as more than the person who so broke your trust. Your old relationship is gone, so take the time to forge a new one with them. Have fun getting to know each other again. Go on dates, just like you did when you first met, and broaden and deepen your understanding of one another through shared conversation, time, and experiences.

Chapter Five:
Dead Bedrooms

When we're young and idealistic, we tend to imagine that sex won't be a problem when we're married. It's easy to assume that when you're married to someone, sex is as frequent and as fulfilling as you could want it to be. While this may be true for some lucky people, for many others it's a bad joke. Millions of people are locked into sexless marriages where despite being married, they get less action than they would if they were single. This nightmarish scenario is all too common, horrible, and difficult to get out of, but it can be done. In this chapter, we'll be examining how.

Sex and Relationships

Sex is a vitally important part of any relationship. In fact, it's a vitally important part of being human. It's one of our most basic and powerful drives, second only to our desire to eat, drink, and sleep. There's a good reason for this: we are the result of millions upon millions of years of evolution where genes have been passed on from one generation to the next through sexual reproduction. If we didn't want sex as much as we do, we wouldn't be here in the first place. We're wired to want it, and we're wired to want it a lot. When we're not sexually fulfilled we don't just crave it, we need it; in a similar way to when we haven't eaten for a few days we're not just hungry, but famished. Sex drives and controls us far more than we might realize. We tend to pick out partners that we have sex with and become highly territorial over them. I'm sure everybody reading or listening to this book knows the acute feeling of jealousy we can get when we even imagine our sexual partner being with someone else instead of us. While relationships vary in style and type right across the world, most people in the west tend to seek and maintain monogamous relationships consisting of two people who are sexually exclusive. While choosing to have a different type of relationship to this is far from uncommon, the default for our western culture is that we pair up, settle down, and become exclusive.

Relationships and sexual satisfaction are therefore fundamentally linked. We rely on our partner to sexually satisfy us. With marriage, this link becomes even further cemented. Even when you're dating, differing libidos can cause couples to break up. It's not so easy to go back once you're married. You're locked in, relatively speaking, and if the sex dries up it isn't as simple as just up and leaving. Additionally, marriage itself seems to be the catalyst for the sex lives of come couples fading away. Why is it that unmarried couples don't seem to have so much of a problem with it when married couples suffer so badly?

The thing is, bad sex lives aren't only limited to marriages. There are plenty of unmarried couples out there who have less (or more!) sex than one or more partners would prefer. Generally speaking, however, people with bad sex lives as unmarried couples don't tend to get married, although when they do it's obvious that marriage isn't the reason for their lack of sex. Marriage itself can cause things to grow stale in the bedroom, however, and there are a number of reasons for this. For one thing, married couples tend to have known each other much longer than unmarried couples. This in itself can be a real problem for the sex life of any couple, because time breeds familiarity and routine and these things are the opposite of novelty, which, as we've already discussed, is a particularly big turn on for men; sex can become boring, predictable and stale simply due to the course of time taking the edge off of things. Sex by its very nature is a hormonal, exciting, spontaneous beast. It's opportunistic and heart-pounding in the wild. When you can set your watch by your marriage's sexual routine, it's no wonder that things start to seem dull. Another common cause of dead bedrooms in marriage is differences in the libido of each spouse. Contrary to what some may think, libidos aren't a rigid and unchanging description of a person's natural appetite to sex. They do tend to have a sort of default range that determines a person's sex drive, but this is prone to waxing and waning according to the circumstances and mindset of an individual throughout the course of their life.

A person's libido at any one point in their life can be influenced by a multitude of different factors. Stress from careers or financial pressure can make it very difficult to think about or focus on sex, or even to desire it in the first place. In the same way, body confidence issues, substance dependence, real or perceived time constraints, and feeling obliged or required to participate in sex can put people off of sex and result in a dead bedroom. Perhaps the single biggest factor for married couples in terms of the decline in the quantity and quality of sex they have is having children. Having kids is a game changer in a multitude of ways, but it can have an inordinate impact on the health of your sex life as a married couple. Having children can hit women especially hard due to the change in hormones that they experience during pregnancy and after birth. It isn't uncommon for women to lose interest in sex completely for a short period of time after they have a child, especially when the stress and pressure of having to look after a newborn and raise children is taken into account. Having children can also interfere in a couple's sex life in a practical way, as many couples are unwilling to shut their bedroom door in case their children want to come in and avoid making too much noise or letting things get too carried away in the moment to stop their children from overhearing.

In some marriages, another contributing factor to the lack of a healthy and fulfilling sex life is the issue of sex being used as a weapon or as a reward. When sex is withdrawn in order to punish or offered in order to persuade, it changes from being a mutually fulfilling and rewarding recreational and intimacy-boosting activity to being a commodity, used as a bargaining chip or withheld in order to curb unwanted behavior. This kind of sexual dynamic is incredibly unhealthy and breeds resentment in a marriage. Treating sex as a commodity changes the fundamental aspect of a relationship from one of togetherness and teamwork to one of conflict and contest. It tarnishes what should be a sacred and special act of intimacy and bonding, warping it into something to be used as a means to an end, rather than an end in and of itself.

Dead bedrooms can be disastrous for a marriage. Not only do the sex lives of our spouses suffer, but when there's a lack of sex there comes a lack of intimacy — and not just in the bedroom. Without sex, married couples drift apart. They become less physically and emotionally close, and can even begin to resemble housemates more than they do a romantic relationship. The cuddling stops. The holding hands and hugging and kissing each other on the cheek stops, and things can go downhill very quickly. Dead bedrooms tend to fuel a vicious cycle where the lack of intimacy and connection that result from the absence of sex makes it very difficult for a couple to reconnect and improve their love life. Once resentment and blaming each other sets in, a rift appears that can further separate a couple and drive them closer to divorce.

Restoring Intimacy in Your Marriage

Bringing a dead bedroom back to life is no easy task, and the most effective method is very much dependent on the problems of each individual marriage. Often, one of the biggest problems that dead bedrooms cause and perpetuate is that sex becomes a huge deal. It turns into the elephant in the room, a focal point and a key area of conflict with a lot riding on it. This can lead to the problem becoming far worse because both parties know it's a big deal and performance anxiety begins to set in.

Sex should be a mutually enjoyable activity that brings you and your spouse closer in your marriage and is shared and appreciated between you. A dead bedroom suggests that this is no longer the status of you and your spouse's sex life, but a lack of sex is more often the symptom of deeper problems in a marriage than it is a self-contained problem. Bringing the sex back so often involves working out what these issues are and addressing them first and foremost, before trying to tackle the issue of sex itself. More often than not, issues surrounding dead bedrooms tend to stem from a lack of good communication. If you can work to improve this by having open, honest, and patient conversations, both in general and on the topic of your sex life, then things should improve. Sort out the main flashpoints first, and with the lessening of conflict should come a thaw in the ice and improve intimacy. Work out the basics of why intimacy has been lost, and keep track of how much sex you're having as a couple in order to objectively assess the state of your sex life and have the difficult conversations necessary to rectify your problems.

You also need to work at creating a mutual desire for sex. It can be easy to classify yourself and your spouse into a high-libido and low-libido dichotomy and then blame each other for your differences in expectation of sex, but things are very rarely as simple as that. Your libido might influence how often you become aroused and desire sex with no prior stimuli, but it doesn't inhibit you from becoming aroused and desiring sex after it has been initiated. If, for example, you have a husband who has a low libido and rarely initiates sex; it doesn't necessarily follow that he doesn't enjoy or wouldn't like to have sex once you've initiated things — only that they don't think to initiate it themselves very often! There needs to be a frank and open discussion about your sex life as a couple, including the expectations each of you have about what your sex life should be like. Marriage is all about compromise, and you need to be able to meet in the middle. Perhaps one of you could be having sex slightly less often than you like, and the other could be having sex slightly more often than they might want. The result is that neither of you 'win' or 'lose'; you work together to come to a solution that works for both of you.

If you or your partner's low libido is an enduring problem, then it's wise to look at what the underlying causes of low libido might be. Perhaps it's a matter of self-esteem or poor self-image, or the taking of antidepressants, or emotional baggage that hasn't been dealt with properly. Whatever the underlying problem might be, working through it may help to improve libidos and enhance the sex life of your marriage.

Creating desire for sex also involves working harder on building up the atmosphere and tension surrounding it. Rather than being born out of a sense of expectation, routine, or duty, work to make sex a fun activity once again. Bring the excitement back! You can spice things up in any number of ways if you use a little bit of imagination. Try to cultivate an atmosphere of excitement and novelty surrounding your sex life by trying new things and shaking it up. There's far more to sex as a married couple than missionary under the sheets with the lights off for all of five minutes.

Quick tip: The best way to create a desire for sex is to work on improving the intimacy of your marriage without any expectation of sex. Hold your spouse's hand, take them on dates, hug them from behind while they do the washing up. Do all of the little loving things that make them feel special for the sake of doing them, not just to try and get sex out of them. Respark your relationship through nice gestures to demonstrate your love and appreciation, and the sex will follow.

Chapter Six:
Handling Emotional Abuse

While any kind of abuse in any context is horrible and wrong, in this book we'll be focusing mainly on emotional abuse in marriages rather than physical abuse. The latter form tends to be more obvious while emotional abuse is far more subtle and insidious; sometimes neither party is even aware that it is taking place. In this chapter, I'll be coaching you how to handle any emotional abuse that you might face in your marriage.

What is Emotional Abuse?

Emotional abuse is sometimes known as psychological abuse. It is something of an umbrella term used to describe a range of behaviors and patterns of repeated conduct that have a serious negative effect on a person's mental health and sense of well-being. While virtually everyone is aware of what physical abuse is owing to its visibility and obvious and dramatic nature, emotional abuse can often fly low under the radar and fall into a grey area in people's judgment where the bigger picture of abuse that certain isolated, negative, toxic patterns of behavior make up isn't clear.

There a number of different elements that make up emotional abuse. Some of these are:

1. **Intimidation and threats** - This refers to any behavior that is intended to manipulate or pressure you into doing what someone wants. It can be small acts of aggression such as shouting (verbal abuse) or acting aggressively, all the way through to breaking things and threatening to hurt you in some way.

2. **Undermining** - This is the act of eroding your position or making you feel small. It includes things like dismissing your opinion, consistently disagreeing with you, and making you look wrong or stupid in front of others.

3. **Gaslighting** - Gaslighting is when someone tries to make you doubt your own opinion or your recollection of past events. They may prod, poke, outright lie, or try to tell you that you're overreacting, being oversensitive, or remembering something wrong.

4. **Attempts to control you** - A person trying to tell you what you can and can't wear, who you can or can't hang out with, what you eat, what you watch on TV, and what you do with your life all counts as them attempting to control

you. Emotionally abusive people seek to order their worlds by keeping the people in their lives on a short leash and under their control.

5. **Economic abuse** - Withholding money, preventing you from getting a job, or excluding you from having finances of your own all count as economic abuse. It's another form of trying to control you by keeping you dependent on your abuser for financial support.

6. **Being made to feel guilty** - Emotionally abusive people use this as a tactic to motivate others to do what they want by making them feel as though they owe the favor to them somehow or that they would be wrong to refuse.

7. **Excessive criticism** - This is especially relevant when it's part of a pattern of potshots aimed at taking down your self-esteem or self-value and self-purpose.

It's important to point out that sometimes a person who is perpetrating emotional abuse isn't even aware that what they're doing is even abusive. Some people lack the self-awareness to step back and look at their own behavior in context, and be able to make a rational judgment about what they've been doing and why. Often, emotionally abusive people are simply used to treating the people in their life that way because they've worked out they can make people do what they want through using emotionally abusive techniques. Nobody deserves abuse, but it's all terrifyingly common. It can be perpetrated by anyone and received by anyone, regardless of social role. People emotionally abuse others for all kinds of reasons, most of which have to do with trying to manipulate and control people, as well as making themselves feel better about themselves by putting other people down. This last reason is normally an opportunistic and often thinly veiled sniping at your own value and worth which makes the people who do it feel slightly better about their own self-image, with which they are seriously unhappy. Think of it like someone who's drowning climbing over someone trying to keep them afloat and pushing them underwater in the process of trying to gasp for air.

Emotional abuse can and often does escalate into physical abuse if left unchecked. After becoming sick and tired of being bullied emotionally, some victims who begin to stand up to their abusers can find themselves being attacked or assaulted as a final attempt to dominate and exert control over them. Emotional abuse has a high correlation with domestic violence and physical abuse, so it is vital that anyone suffering from it seeks as much help as possible in order to deal with the problem.

Dealing With Emotional Abuse

Although there are some who may disagree, it has been my experience that the majority of emotionally abusive people aren't actually bad people at heart, although when it comes to physical abuse it becomes harder to make excuses. There are a lot of people out there who never really learn the right way to talk to others or fail to recognize the full consequences of their words beyond their own self interest. Regardless of this, safety should always be the primary concern when trying to handle emotional abuse. It's okay to stand up for yourself, speak up, and get yourself out of the situation you're in. You're entitled to be treated with respect. You deserve better than living under the thumb of somebody else, but be smart, protect yourself, and make sure you get out of that situation. You have to be brave and put yourself first to avoid people taking advantage of you in life.

There are two main approaches towards handling emotional abuse. If the abuse isn't particularly bad, it might be able to be broken by using communication strategies in order to try and reach the other person and show them the effect that their actions and words are having on you. Sitting them down and having a difficult but open and honest conversation about things as you see them might be enough to open someone's eyes as to the true nature of their behavior. Keep in mind that doing this can cause people to become defensive and aggressive, however, so it might be best to do it somewhere relatively public. Another strategy than can be very effective is to first identify emotional abuse, verify it, and then accept it. You can practice this method by picking out when you're on the receiving end of emotional abuse and then flagging it up to your abuser by asking them why they said or did something. Regardless of whether their response is to deflect or be defensive, you can then tell them how what they said or did made you feel and ask them if their intention was to make you feel that way. You then accept whatever their response is and try to reach them by opening their eyes momentarily on the spot right after they've done something negative or toxic. You can then gain an understanding of their motivations and a revelation about their true character and self-awareness. Doing this can help you to curb an abusive person's behavior by more slowly showing them that you understand why they're doing something and that it's hurting you; it can also give you the green light to extract yourself from their lives and make your own way on your own terms. It's a slower approach, but it can be more effective at defusing a person and slowly helping them to change their ways rather than forcing an intervention by having an open and honest discussion about it.

Another method is something known as 'grey rocking'. This technique essentially involves curbing emotionally abusive behavior by withholding the emotional response that they're looking for. This is particularly effective within the context of verbal abuse and criticism, where you have total control over how you respond. If you remain as neutral and as calm and withdrawn from the situation as possible without provoking them, they will eventually begin to get bored with abusing you emotionally as there isn't the satisfying effect of seeing you become upset or snapping back at them. When you don't give an emotionally abusive person the response they're looking for, you're depriving them of their motivation to do it in the first place.

Chapter Seven: Saving Your Marriage

At this stage in the book, it's time to put everything together and knuckle down in order to address the ultimate question: how do you save your marriage?

Prevent Divorce and Save Your Marriage

Virtually all of us come to a point in our marriage where we have a tough decision to make. Do we give up on things and call it a day, or do we knuckle down and save our marriage? If the former decision is yours, then the next chapter will deal with how to go about putting that into process. I myself am a big advocate of preserving marriages, saving the key relationships in your life, and enriching the bonds you have with people in order to push on together and help each other to a better future. I think we have to work together as a team in order to learn and grow in the right way. Nobody is perfect, and everyone makes mistakes. Every marriage has room for improvement, and you have to work hard in order to be fulfilled and happy with your spouse and they with you. I say stick by them, if you can — but only when both of you being happy and fulfilled together is an option. Never stay with someone if you're only going to be miserable with them.

It's never too late to save your marriage. As I've mentioned previously in this book, I've seen couples who had gone through a whole carnival of carnage throughout the course of their marriage, done each other the world of hurt and had extremely bitter feelings and lots of resentment towards each other come out on the other side of their marriage difficulty as happy, well-adjusted, enlightened and loving people, aware of the true nature of the difficulties of being married and being human and determined to stick together and face life alongside one another rather than going their separate ways. Saving your marriage is an incredibly educational and humbling experience. There's not much quite like it in terms of changing your perspective and the way you think and feel. You become aware of just how much difficulty both you and your spouse are facing in life, and through communication come to understand, accept, and love each other once again.

Saving your marriage is a relatively straightforward — although not easy — process. It's all about making an honest assessment of the direction, velocity, and character of your marriage, and then making a concerted effort alongside your spouse to improve and elevate them. You need to work out what you're doing right as a couple and where you're going wrong, and then try to do more of what works and less of what doesn't. The attitude, mindset and assumptions with which you approach your marriage will determine whether you make it a fulfilling and satisfying part of your life or allow it to be draining and toxic. How you deal with problems makes far more of a difference in your marriage than the nature of the problems themselves.

Everybody is unique, so there are always differences in relationships, no matter how similar to someone else you might feel. Our differences are a good thing — they're essential and interesting, and tell us about who we are as people. However, differences create conflict. How you deal with this conflict is the measure of whether you make or break a marriage. Every relationship experiences conflict from time to time, but how do you treat it? Is it raised voices and regretful comments or calm, understanding, patient dialogue? The choice is yours.

Marriages tend to have a certain tornado-like structure, which is often the result of the chaos we experience in childhood. There is a calm middle ground in the center where we can be together and be level, but as soon as an issue is pushed too far in any one direction the conflict and pain starts. This setup only inevitably leads to hurt and leaves us balancing precariously in the eye of the storm because we're afraid that doing anything to rock the boat might throw everything off kilter and ruin a hard-won peace. This is the height of neuroticism, but it's part of being human. In general, we lack the understanding and perspective to really be part of a happy and fulfilling life partnership with others. It's only through working hard to change the whole dynamic of your marriage and relationship to one another that you can extract yourselves from this tornado-like system and really begin to appreciate what it means to live life by each other's side.

When you're experiencing difficulty in your marriage, the first thing you have to recognize, accept, and work on is that you're no longer each other's first priority. Somewhere along the line, the marriage has developed in such a way that you've grown further apart than you once were. There's a lack of connection and importance, and you lose each other's hearts. The critical moment when you have this realization as a couple can either be the day the divorce effectively and symbolically happens or the day you decide that you're going to stop this process of losing each other's hearts and work to win them back.

In order to win each other back, you have to think in terms of why you're losing or have lost the connection you had that made you want to get married in the first place or made the two of you fall in love. You have lost somewhere the intimacy in your marriage along the way, and it needs to return. The problem with this is that it can't just be found like a lost object; once it's gone, the only way to get it back is to rebuild it the slow way you did it in the first place. You need to talk to each other in depth about your feelings and the way you experience life. About why you are the way you are and the reasons behind you doing the things you do. You need to go back over the issues that have been molding you from childhood and work out how to move on from the things that have held you back. Part of reconnecting as a couple is bringing the problems you both face out of the subconscious and exposing it to the light. Try to become aware of the reasons why you are the way you are, rather than living your life in misery and ignorance. Just talking about these problems with one another will weaken the hold they have over you, helping you to leave them in the past where they belong.

Sometimes, we don't even remember the influential and traumatic past events that shape us and determine the way we treat ourselves and others. This unconscious programming can often only be uncovered by talking about it. You have to start talking about things for the domino effect to start and things to begin coming back to you and make sense in the wider context of molding you into the person you are today. We have to first examine our own wiring in this way to really begin to change it. Raising your own and your spouse's awareness of the programming you received from childhood, especially from upsetting and traumatic events, is absolutely vital to becoming more well-adjusted people and having a better marriage relationship. Without talking about the things that have happened to you at length or in detail, you're just not able to truly process and deal with them You have to open up in order to let things out and release their control over you. It's the difference between dealing with the source and root of the problem or merely treating the symptoms. When you learn to overcome your subconscious programming, it becomes easier to look at things objectively and tackle them together, rather than just blaming each other for your problems.

The deeper the conversation gets in any relationship, the closer the people in it become. The more you talk about your problems with your spouse, the more the two of you will reconnect. As the two of you talk, you should make a mutual commitment to changing the nature of your marriage. It's very important that you're both on the same page about this. You need to both want to make your marriage a happy, balanced, fulfilling thing to be a part of. For that, you both need to understand how to go about doing this and be prepared to put in the work to make it so. Learning to look at things positively is of paramount importance, as is understanding that nothing is ever perfect and that there is always more to be done. Like anything in life, having a great marriage is a matter of choice. Although it's only once you see that it's a choice that it becomes one. Your attitude towards and position on your marriage influence where you look and how you compare your own married relationship to that of other married couples. This is also known as selection bias. If you feel like your marriage is awful, you will be far more likely to take note of and compare your marriage to another one when the other seems better than yours. In the same way, feeling good about your marriage makes you more likely to compare it to poorer marriages. In truth, every marriage is good and bad. It is what it is. It could always be better, it could always be worse — and that's the way things will always be.

It's essential that you begin the healing process as soon as you can — ideally before you fall out of love completely, although it is almost always possible to claw back to it with enough hard work; the problem with falling out of love is that it removes the motivation to work hard on your marriage in the first place, as it no longer seems to be worth it. Whatever stage you and your spouse are at, keep in mind that these things take time. There's no quick or easy fix when it comes to relationships. You have to just consistently put the work in and see how things pan out in the long run. Divorce is a permanent solution to a temporary problem, so try to keep in mind the bigger picture that you're aiming for and remember to try and see all of the positivity and beauty that exists in your marriage *right now*, and all the good things that you and your spouse could do and create in the near future once you're back on track. This attitude and proactivity in demonstrating how much your spouse means to you is what will keep your marriage alive, even if it's on life support.

There's a stark contrast between doing what is easy and doing what is right. Doing the right thing as one half of a married couple is rarely ever easy, but that doesn't mean that you have an excuse not to do it. Being married is a difficult enterprise, but it's richly rewarding as long as you're willing to do what the work to make it that way. Marriage has to be intimate and highly involved to work; otherwise, you won't enjoy touching, talking, or being around each other. Only the right attitude, principles, values, and outlooks can generate this intimacy being shared and expressed by both you and your spouse. Try to bring inspiration and energy to your marriage. Be creative. Seek to build things together, not destroy them. Use your thoughts, use your language, and use your trust to steer the two of you in the right direction.

Saving Your Marriage Alone

Marriage is a team sport. If you're not working together in at least some capacity or there's some willingness from both sides to save the marriage, it's not going to work. That being said, there are times when one person is far more invested in saving a marriage than their spouse is, and is placed in the impossible position of having to try to make it work all by themselves. Although it does take two to tango, there are often valid reasons why one spouse is willing to put in much more effort than their partner that aren't because they're totally uninterested and want things to end. People are incredibly complicated and impossibly complex. Picking apart how you feel and why you feel that way is a difficult thing to do, and sometimes we just get lost in limbo where nothing seems to mean anything. That doesn't mean that we'll feel that way forever.

If you feel like your spouse isn't doing as much or isn't as interested in saving your marriage as you are, you're put in a challenging situation. Obviously, it's one that can't last forever. You can't carry your marriage single-handedly for the rest of your lives, nor should you want to. Maneuvering out of this place involves getting your partner back on board and engaged by acting unilaterally and making sure that you are doing all that you can do to make things better between you. If even after you've demonstrated what your marriage means to you and how hard you're willing to fight for it your spouse still shows little interest in putting in more effort to make things better, it might be a lost cause. In the meantime, all you can do is try.

The first thing to accept when it comes to saving your marriage on your own is that your spouse is already putting in all they're going to put in for the time being. There's no quick fix or easy way to get them engaged and fighting for your marriage. No, it's not fair, and yes, they should do more, but in all probability, if they haven't done so already then they will not start any time soon. There is nothing you can do to change or control them or make them take things seriously. Any attempts to do so will likely only make things between the two of you worse. Instead, you'll have to focus on knuckling down, getting into the trenches, and doing the heavy lifting yourself, for now. You're getting all you can out of your spouse currently, so it will have to be enough until they come around and start pulling their weight.

The process of saving your marriage single-handedly doesn't deviate too much from the rest of the advice I've already laid out throughout this book. The difference is that you have to be far more committed and driven in order to do these things by yourself without your partner doing the same thing. You will become fed up and disillusioned. You will wonder why you ever even try. But if you persist and hang in there, your positivity, love, kindness, and effort will begin to rub off on your partner. After all, the best way to get the two of you out of the quicksand is sometimes to work to free yourself first and then come back to help. The attitudes and behavior of the people around us rub off on us, so if you can put the ideas we've discussed in this book to work single-handedly, you will more likely than not be able to bring your partner around to seeing things from a healthier, more positive point of view.

Gratitude and positivity give you the power and the perspective you need to be able to push on and tackle everything else. They will also help to cultivate the same characteristics in your partner. As human beings, we're naturally hard-wired to evaluate everything in our lives. This means that we tend to judge things simply as a force of habit. However, this judgment is a choice and something that we can reconsider to develop an attitude of openness and interest without jumping to negative conclusions straight away. A lot of marriages feature something known as 'blame outsourcing', where we judge and place the blame for our problems on our partners when really we have at least a contributory role to all of the issues in our life. This might be the case for you or your spouse; it's likely that there's an element of this in both of your attitudes towards each other. Understanding this can help us to take responsibility for our problems and focus on doing what we can and should to do hold up our end of the deal, keep our vows, and do everything we can to save our marriage, even if that means acting alone at first.

The Pressure of Having Children

One of the most central elements of most marriages and a common cause of stress, pressure, and conflict is having children. Even before a child is conceived, the very concept of one can put a serious strain on any relationship. Having a baby is a significant economic, time, and social investment, and for this reason issues of practicality and timing inevitably surface. Even within the context of a marriage, the topic of having children can be a difficult subject. It's for this reason that it's so important that both you and your spouse are as clear as you can be about your own and each other's expectations when it comes to having children to avoid disappointment if they significantly differ.

Having children changes a relationship in a number of deep and fundamental ways. If you have kids, then it's important that you compensate for the effect they inevitably have on your marriage in order to keep it healthy and happy. They bring a vast amount of pressure and stress into the relationship dynamic between their caregivers, who have to make sure they provide their children with food, clothes, quality time, love, and the stimulation that they need to grow and develop in a healthy manner. The combined effect of all of this can put a lot of strain on even the strongest marriage.

Every relationship needs maintenance, especially during times of change. Having a child is possibly the most extraordinary and boundary-pushing experience a person can have, so it's even more important that you give your marriage the time and effort it deserves, rather than neglecting it to focus your attention on your children. It's incredibly easy to become absorbed by our children; after all, we're genetically coded to put them before ourselves in every way. You have to maintain the other relationships in your life, though, and very few of these are more important than the one you have with your spouse. Make sure you're taking time for your marriage and attempting to spend time alone with your spouse. This might mean having someone else watch the kids while the two of you go out for a date night together, or simply making the effort to cuddle, kiss, and watch a movie together after the kids have gone to sleep. You need to spend time together as a couple to remember that you're not just parents; you're married. You're lovers, best friends, and better halves first and foremost, although it can be easy to lose sight of this. Make sure you take the time to rekindle things from time to time and allow yourselves to be comfortable just being alone and spending time together to maintain the strength of your marriage and the bond you have with each other.

Another important thing to do to keep your marriage strong when you have children is to remember to take care of yourself. If your own immediate needs aren't met, how can you expect to be a good husband, wife, or parent? The single most important relationship we have in life is the one we have with ourselves. If you're not doing the things you need to do to look after yourself, then your marriage will inevitably suffer, along with every other aspect of your life. It can be very hard to remember to take the time to be alone and do the things that you enjoy doing, the things that revive and refresh you and leave you feeling revitalized. A common side effect of having children is feeling less individual, less like an autonomous human being, and more like the social role you have to play for your family. Everyone needs their alone time, time spent doing what they love and seeing their friends. Without this, the relationships in our lives inevitably suffer. If you want to save your marriage, then make sure both you and your spouse are taking time for yourselves.

Quick tip: You're not in this alone. Everybody needs a support network, people around them to enjoy life with when things are good and to help share the burden when times get rough. Your spouse and children represent a great support network for you, but make sure that you don't neglect yourself or your friends while enjoying family life. Through you and your spouse remembering to spend time on each other and yourselves, you will help to cultivate a peaceful, caring, loving home environment for everyone in your family.

Bonus: Date Night Ideas for Married Couples

When it comes to spending quality time with your spouse, you're not just taking time to enjoy yourselves. You're reconnecting as a couple. You're strengthening the bond and the intimacy that the two of you share, and these will be the factors that enable you to go the distance together. Besides, you only live your life once. You have to have fun and enjoy yourself, and who better to share recreational activities with than the person you married because you wanted to spend the rest of your life with them?

I'd recommend making at least one allocated night of the week date night, such as Friday or Saturday, and sticking to it every week as far as you possibly can. This gives the two of you something to look forward to at the end of the week and ensures that you're consistently spending quality time together. You can also talk about and plan what you're going to do every weekend throughout the course of the week, which builds tension and excitement and ensures you're always coming up with fun ideas.

While part of the fun of having a weekly date night is planning what to do with your spouse or being spontaneous, I've included a few ideas to help get you started:

1. **Dinner and a movie** - This is a classic, but it's a classic for good reason. Going out for a romantic dinner with your spouse before heading to see a movie at the cinema makes for a fun, intimate date night. It's a good mix of conversation and passive entertainment where you can sit back, relax, and enjoy a show together while holding hands. You can even extend it afterwards before going home by going for a walk or a drive somewhere together. All in all, I always vouch for this as one of the top date ideas of all time. It's versatile, effective, and thoroughly enjoyable, plus you get to eat a nice meal and then have popcorn and a soda.

2. **Going for drinks** - This is another classic. There's nothing quite like kicking back at the bar or in the privacy of a booth and getting a bit too drunk with your spouse. After all, dates are about having fun, and drinking certainly facilitates that! You can have hours and hours of conversation, flirting, and building intimacy with nothing but the two of you and a handful of drinks each. Alcohol can really help to break the ice, too, especially if the two of you have been going through a rough patch and aren't sure how to go about rebuilding the intimacy. Going for drinks can also take you back to when you were dating, and all of the excitement and anticipation that comes along with it. Just make sure you have a ride home!

3. **Bowling** - Playing games together is a lot of fun. You can laugh, joke, and innocently poke fun at each other in a

way that really builds the camaraderie and intimacy between the two of you. Being married is about being great friends, and fun activities like bowling are an excellent way to maintain your friendship or spice things up and remind yourselves of who you are to each other when you've been feeling distant.

4. **Going to the beach** - This is an often overlooked but extremely rewarding date experience in my opinion — provided you're near a beach. You can go during the day when it's warm and swim and sunbathe or read or listen to music while eating ice cream together, or at night with some blankets and look at the stars while listening to the waves rolling in. This kind of date is especially magical if it's not the kind of thing you'd normally do together, just the two of you. It evokes the feeling of being young and in love all

over again, something that I know many marriages are sorely lacking.

5. **Dessert** - Going for dessert together is a great, if short, date idea, particularly fulfilling if it's spur of the moment or you've already been doing something together. It's a great way to top off the evening and spend some time reflecting on what you've done previously, although it's a solid standalone date idea in itself; especially if the place you get dessert packs a serious punch.

6. **Theatre** - Much like going to the movies, going to the theatre with your spouse is a recipe for a brilliant date. You also have the added bonus of an interlude and the novelty of seeing actors performing live, something that can be an incredibly powerful and moving

experience. If you have the opportunity to go and see one of the big Broadway-esque musicals you should jump at it; they're mind blowingly good fun and will have the two of you talking about it together for days afterwards. Dates like this allow you to do something before and/or after too, meaning you can tailor the experience to get as much out of it as you desire.

7. **Outdoor activities** - These may not be everyone's idea for a great date, but for some people they're magical. You should try to allocate whole days to things like this rather than evenings. There's something about being out in the wilderness hiking on a trail with your spouse, or riding bikes, or taking a boat out on a lake together that inspires overwhelming feelings of love, gratitude,

and appreciation. Spending time together in the great outdoors is a humbling and intimate experience, if you're that way inclined. It doesn't have to be anything dramatic or intense, either. You could go for a picnic together, or even a walk. Fresh air and the company of your spouse are all you really need for a great date, sometimes.

8. **Going on vacation** - Whether you finally decide to take that trip to Europe or you're not traveling that far, taking a trip somewhere with your spouse is a very personal and thoroughly fulfilling thing to do. It places the emphasis for both of you on hanging out and spending leisure time together for days at a time, giving you a break from ordinary working life and providing you with a

chance to relax together and get to know one another all over again.

9. **Game nights** - A lot of people shrink from the idea of game nights as a way to have fun, but I've always found them to be brilliant. Whether you get a good two-player game or you meet up with other couples and friends for a group activity, playing games is an excellent way to build intimacy and bond with your spouse.

10. **Quiet nights in** - Sometimes, all you need to have fun is the pleasure of each other's company and a night at home together. I find that the simplest dates are often the most rewarding, and spending quality time together can be as simple or as complicated as you want to make it. Nights in can be especially

rewarding when one of you cooks for the other, or you cook a meal together and share a bottle of wine, some dessert, and a movie. Being in the comfort of your own home can really add to the atmosphere, too.

Chapter Eight:
Divorce

You probably wouldn't be reading or listening to this book if you were certain you wanted a divorce, but I want this to be a totally inclusive guide, and a handbook for saving marriage wouldn't be complete without a caveat about how to go about ending it the right way. It's a shame, but all things must come to an end one way or another, and sometimes people just aren't meant to be together. If your mind lingers on thoughts about separating from your spouse or they seem to have it in mind themselves, then this chapter is for you.

When Should You Get Divorced?

The question of when it's right to stay and fight for your marriage and when it's best to cut your losses and call it a day is a difficult one to answer. As I've previously mentioned, I am a big advocate of married couples remaining together if they possibly can, if they can find a way to make things work between them and be happy and fulfilled together, and I maintain that most couples can — far more than actually do so. Throwing in the towel is the easy way out, and as the sky-high divorce rates for remarried people goes to show, staying married is far more a process of tenacity and persistence than it is about marrying the right person in the first place. Willpower is everything, and with enough drive and a little guidance virtually any couple can learn how to make their marriage work. Sometimes, however, this just isn't the case. Life tends unfold in the strangest of ways, and many, if not most married people at some point find thoughts of getting divorced coming to them all too readily.

You're not wrong for considering divorce, nor would you be wrong to go through with the process. At the end of the day, the most important thing in your life is you own happiness and well-being, and you have to do whatever you need to protect that. You know the details of your marriage better than anyone, along with your spouse. If you're convinced that there's nothing there worth saving, or you don't want to save it, then you should honor those feelings. Life is too short to be unhappy. You'll know if divorce is the right call or if there's still something between you and your spouse that's worth fighting for. Sometimes people just don't end up working well together; when happiness together becomes an unattainable pipe dream, regardless of the attitude and mindset and willingness to try and improve things from each half of the couple, then it's probably game over, unless you'd prefer to spend the rest of your life in misery.

Deciding whether or not you should get divorced is never something that should be taken lightly. I'd recommend trying to get all the space and perspective you can when you're trying to make up your mind. If you can get out of the house for a few days, or find some other way to have less contact with your spouse other than for essential purposes for a short while, you may find it helps to shift the way you see things and more thoroughly understand what it is that you want from your life, and whether or not your spouse can be a part of that. Talking things through with close friends and family is also a great idea as it can help you to work out how you truly think and feel about your marriage and whether you want to hang in there and try to make things work or you're ready to move on. If you believe that the time is right to draw a line under everything and get a divorce, then that is what you should do. You have to trust yourself and your own judgment; you have to believe in yourself and have your own back. If you won't stand up for yourself and your own happiness and well-being and do what's right for you, then who will?

What to do When Your Spouse Wants to Divorce

If you're in a situation where your spouse has told you that they want to get a divorce, the first thing that you need to do is take a deep breath and try to stay calm. It isn't the end of the world. Keep breathing, stay out of crisis mode. If you start to panic, you'll slip into fight-or-flight mode which will impede your ability to think calmly and clearly. Now, the next few steps you take depends entirely on the full context of your situation; your marriage, the way your spouse feels about your marriage, and the way you feel about it. Perhaps you will end up getting divorced, but maybe you won't. Just because your spouse is saying they want one doesn't necessarily mean that it will end up being what the two of you decide to do. Nothing is set in stone. If you do end up getting divorced, it will be because that course of action is the best for both of you. Whatever happens, your future will be full of happiness and laughter and joy because you possess the power to make it so.

What needs to happen next is important but not urgent, so take the time to process things and get your mind straight before you jump into the next phase. Firstly, you need to try and make an accurate assessment of the reality of your marriage situation. Does your spouse really want a divorce? How do you know? Do you want to get divorced? How do you know? Talk to your spouse about it as openly, honestly, calmly, and maturely as the two of you can possibly manage, and get everything out in the open. This is make or break, so lay all of the cards you're holding out on the table and encourage your spouse to do the same. Focus on what is wrong, not who is wrong. There's obviously something that's not working, or you wouldn't be in this situation, so it's time to get to the bottom of what is broken and why. Tell your spouse exactly how you feel and what you'd like to do in order to proceed, and ask them to do the same. It may be that your spouse really *wants* to make things work, but is at the end of their tether and feels like perhaps divorce might be the only option. How this interaction goes and the conclusions that you come to as a couple will be determined by your individual situation and the context of your marriage. It might be that the two of you agree to give one another chance to change things, to take one last shot at really making your marriage work.

If, for whatever reason — be it their decision or a mutual one — the two of you are headed for divorce, then the most important thing that you can do is to accept the reality of the situation. If there's nothing more to be done and one or both minds have been made up, then it is what it is. You simply have to accept that things don't always work out the way you might have once thought they would, and that that's okay. It's sad, but it's necessary. If there was another way out, the two of you would have taken it, but this is the end of the line for your marriage. Give yourself as much time and space as you need in order to process this. It might feel like your life is over and the world is ending, but I sincerely promise you that it's not. This might be the end of the current chapter, but it's far from the end of your story; it's the beginning of a whole new chapter. It doesn't matter how old you are, or how afraid you are that you'll never find love again. You can and will find whatever it is that you want to find from the future. No one deserves to be unhappy, so take comfort in the fact that at least that is coming to an end. You wouldn't be in the position you're in if it wasn't for a whole lot of unhappiness, whether that was on your part or your spouse's.

Sometimes, things just don't work out, and marriage is no exception to this. The very best thing you can do is frame the divorce in your mind as one big learning experience. While it's far from a desirable thing to be going through, it will teach you important lessons about yourself, others, and life that you can take forward with you to become a more well-rounded and experienced person. The difficulties we face in life serve to reveal to us exactly who we are and teach us fundamental lessons about what it means to be human. If you can see the beauty in that, you can take all of the positives (and there will be positives, no matter how hard that may be to believe) from your divorce forwards with you while learning all you can from the negatives and then letting them go to move on with your life in a whole new direction.

Don't fall into the trap of thinking that your main priority should be to find someone else, fast. Getting divorced, like all things in life, is an opportunity. It's a chance to figure out more about who you are and embrace all the things you want to do in life that you might not have been as easily able to do when you were married. Personal development is the inevitable result of any relationship coming to an end, and should strive to embrace this wholeheartedly. There are many, many people stuck in miserable marriages that they can't escape from, and no matter the context of your own marriage, you at least have the freedom to live life on your own terms and make the most out of the time you have to appreciate the incredible experience we call life.

Divorcing Peacefully

Once it's clear that divorce is inevitable, the only thing that's left to do is try to get through the whole process as civilly and amicably as you possibly can. Once the path of divorce has been chosen by one of you, both of you are on it, regardless of whether or not you want to be. If it was your choice to split up, then own it; if this is truly what you want, then don't cave. If it wasn't your choice, all you can do is accept the path you're on and try to make things as easy for both of you as possible. Divorces can get messy fast, especially when it comes to things like finances and custody of children if you have any. Just because your marriage is ending doesn't mean the process has to be full of resentment, bitterness, and hostility. Try to look at it as the final problem that you'll have to work together as a team on. It's possible to do it sensibly and maturely and compassionately as long as you exercise self control and don't do anything intentionally malicious. Just because things are coming to an end doesn't mean spite or nastiness has to be a part of it. All you can do is control your own reactions and conduct, so make sure you're always the bigger person if your soon to be ex seems intent on not playing fair.

Do your best to make the divorce a blameless process, if at all possible. You can only do you part in this, of course, but by avoiding placing blame on your spouse you won't be antagonizing them or provoking a legal shoving match. Focus on the bigger picture; your future once this is all said and done, when the process of getting divorced is just a distant memory far over the horizon in the rear-view mirror. Ugly divorces are very rarely planned. They're most often the result of the situation becoming a quagmire of bad feelings and game-playing, where retaliation for real or perceived unfairness provokes a tit for tat dynamic that quickly spirals out of control and ruins any chance for things to proceed amicably. You always have a choice as to how you act and react. If you act in good faith, with dignity and respect for yourself and your spouse, then the chances are good that your spouse will return the gesture and any ugliness can be averted. Getting divorced is a difficult enough process in the first place; there's no reason to make it any harder than it needs to be.

Some of the best advice I can give to anyone going through a divorce is to get a lawyer, delete Facebook, and hit the gym. There are a number of reasons why this combination is so effective at helping the process along and making everything much easier to deal with. For one, your lawyer will deal with any and all legal formalities, providing you with a degree of separation and invaluable expertise that helps you to avoid the messier and more complicated parts of a divorce, especially if you're trying to make it a peaceful separation but your ex-spouse isn't on board with this. Getting off of social media will help you to clear your head. Going through a divorce comes with a lot of social fallout, and steering clear of social media allows you to avoid getting hung up on anything and instead just focus on your own life. After the dust settles, anyone you still want to keep in your life will still be a part of it, social media or not, and everyone else will be in the past where they belong.

As I previously mentioned, perhaps the stickiest area when it comes to divorce is the matter of children, if you have any with your ex. Who gets custody, what the visitation rights are, and things like child support can become a minefield. Having a lawyer will help you out massively with such complicated legal procedures, but in order to make the process of divorce as easy and as peaceful as possible I'd recommend thinking very deeply about the broader context of the situation and what the fairest thing is for your children. You should always try to put them first, in any situation, even if what is best for them isn't what's best for you. Trying to remain friends, or at least on somewhat positive terms with your ex-spouse is also important if you have children, because to some extent you will continue to be involved in each other's lives for matters of cooperative parenting. This isn't possible in every case, obviously, but you should strive for it as far as you can in order to make things easier in the long run.

Moving On

Learning how to move on after going through a divorce can be a very confusing and even overwhelming process. There will be many things that you have to come to grips with, lots of different areas of your life that you must think about for the first time in a long time. You'll feel a whole range of emotions, from being happy and relieved that your marriage is over, particularly if you were unhappy for a long time, to desperately sad, anxious, confused, and alone. Throughout this process, it's crucial that you focus on yourself as an individual, and do the things that you need to do to encourage your own personal development and set yourself up for a better future. Moving on from divorce is a process of recovery. It's about learning how to be on your own again. It's a tough process, but you'll get through it with time, and emerge on the other side a better, wiser person for having had the experience.

An important step towards recovery is understanding what went wrong. Why you married in the first place, and why you ended up getting divorced. Everyone makes mistakes; what's important is that you learn from them. Lots of people get caught up in this process, lingering on questions like 'what did I do wrong?' 'Whose fault is all this?' and 'Why is this happening to me?' But I think the only way to really move on is to realize that it's no one's fault, that no one is to blame, and that life is simply one big learning experience. It's only once you can put the feeling of having to have something to blame and hate for your negative experiences to bed that you can finally begin to see life for what it truly is. It just is. There doesn't have to be a rhyme or reason. It can be helpful to instead focus on what the relationship was lacking and the ways that you and your ex were incompatible just because of who you are. There are problems in every relationship, and they ended up being too much for yours. That's okay. No one is to blame. Your marriage was lacking something and failed to meet you or your spouse's needs in some way. It's better to contemplate questions along this line and look at the whole thing objectively, rather than focusing on who did what and whose fault everything is. Looking at things this way might be more upsetting, but it will help you to gain a clearer understanding of the truth of the situation. The greater your understanding, the easier it will be for you to move on.

The period just after separation and divorce is a chance to reflect, to take an inventory of your life so far and find out where your trajectory is headed, and think about how to change it if you so desire. It's a chance to get your head straight, to find your individuality and work out what kind of person you really want to be, on no one else's terms except your own. Looking after yourself and committing to good habits is vital at this stage, as the first few months are when the reality of the situation really sets in and the time that you will feel most lost and directionless. Your self-esteem and self-confidence may take a hard knock during this time, so it's essential that you do the following things in order to get back up from being knocked down:

1. **Grieve**: A divorce is a massively traumatic life event. So much changes and you're left feeling very different to how you might have been not that long ago. Give yourself the time you need to grieve for the part of your life that has ended, regardless of whether or not you wanted it to. It takes time for reality to settle in and for you to get used to the way things will be from now on. You'll have good days and bad days, so support yourself by allowing yourself to feel the negative emotions you're experiencing.

2. **Let go:** In order to truly move on with your life, you have to come to terms with everything that has happened and allow yourself to let go. The pain and anger you feel can make you feel powerful and strong; they're almost addictive in this sense. Feel how you feel, and honor how

you feel, but then when it's time, let go. The more strongly you hold onto your negative emotions, the harder it will be to sever the connection you have to your past and really move on.

3. **Talk to people:** Not only will talking to people help you to process your thoughts and feelings, but it will also prevent isolation and help you to maintain a healthy sense of perspective. You're not alone. Sharing your inner world with the people you're close with will enable you to better cope with the situation you're in.

4. **Set yourself goals:** Some days it might feel like you're going nowhere fast, and that's okay. I find it can be helpful to plan ahead and set yourself some short term goals in order to give yourself a

schedule to stick to and things to keep you occupied. Make sure any targets you set yourself are achievable, and don't hold it against yourself if you fail to meet all of them.

5. **Look after yourself:** Make sure that you're getting enough sleep each night, eating healthily, and getting enough exercise. If you're not taking good care of yourself, you'll begin to feel more depressed, lethargic, and negative about your life.

6. **Seek help:** If you need help, never be ashamed to ask for it. Friends, therapists, counselors — there are plenty of options for you to speak to people and get real help when you're struggling. You don't have to suffer alone.

One of the things people struggle particularly hard with in the divorce's wake is a sense of loss and failure. This feeling can strike particularly hard if you've experienced some kind of reduction in your standard of living or quality of life after your divorce, such as having to move to a smaller house or apartment or even staying on somebody's couch. At such moments, the world can seem to shrink around you, and the feeling of loss of the sense of safety and security that you once had and now don't can threaten to overwhelm you. This feeling can also strike when you realize that the family dynamic has changed when you're with your kids and your ex-spouse isn't there or you wake up to an empty house without them. It's helpful to remember at times like this that things will get better and you won't always feel this way. We tend to look back on the past with rose-tinted glasses, especially when it's something we miss. Your situation isn't the worst thing that could happen to you, and it's far better than being trapped in an unhappy marriage.

Quick tip: With time, your situation and outlook *will* improve. You'll have a better place from which to get your perspective and feel more familiar with your new lease of life. You'll find love again, in time, and with the lessons you've learned, you'll be able to avoid repeating the mistakes of the past. Being optimistic for the future can be hard, but if you can focus on reclaiming your individuality and living your life the way you want to live then you will feel better about things.

Final Words

Being married and getting divorced are things that more and more of us are going through as we move slowly into the 21st century. I think that now, more than ever, it's essential that we have a clear idea of the difficulties involved in maintaining a lifelong commitment to another person, and just how hard it can be to make things work. Too many people enter into marriage with the idea that things are going to be relatively easy, because they have a mindset of 'it's us' or the idea that they will somehow be exempt from something that married people almost unanimously agree is extremely hard work. I wrote this book because I like to help people. It's the reason I've been practicing as a therapist for so long. I wanted to condense my thoughts and experiences of coaching people through how to stay together and how to begin to address life once more after splitting up.

It's my belief that virtually every marriage can be saved, as long as both partners are willing to try. At their core, all these things really require are dedication and hard work. I make a strong exception for abusive or otherwise extremely unhappy marriages — there are circumstances under which making things work is either an impossible or unattractive prospect — but for most people, in regular, run-of-the-mill marriages with their fair share of ups and downs, making their marriage work is simply a matter of attitude and mindset. From my professional experience, I've learned that there truly is no mountain too high to climb, no obstacle too difficult to overcome. I've seen couples go through hell, go through the worst drama and most horrible experiences that you can imagine, and emerge on the other side stronger for having been through the ordeal. No matter what has happened in the past, there is nothing that can't be put right in the present if both partners are on the same page about wanting to do this.

Teamwork is everything in relationships, and this is especially true in marriage. The lawful act of union represents the pinnacle of intimacy and closeness. As human beings, each of us has an entire world, a whole universe of feelings and thoughts inside of us. Sharing that in such an incredibly intimate and vulnerable way is an extremely difficult thing to do, especially when it means having the difficult conversations that we might not want to have. Who can say why we go through the multitude of difficult circumstances that we do? Things seem to happen to us almost by accident, with us not realizing the true significance of the things we're doing until we're knee-deep in a situation we never imagined we could become stuck in before.

This is why it's so important to be kind and compassionate in our marriages and elsewhere in life. Life unfolds in the strangest of ways, and if we can't be totally open and honest with the person we've pledged our life to, then who? Who can we turn to in our darkest moments when we've made terrible mistakes and desperately in need of forgiveness? It isn't easy, but nothing ever is. We have to be able to keep the bigger picture in mind and forgive each other for our wrongs. We have to be able to sit down and work out how we're going to get through this, rather than pointing fingers and playing the blame game every time someone slips up.

We have to be honest to ourselves and our spouses, no matter how hard that might be. We have to be capable of rebuilding trust when it's broken. We have to be able to understand and forgive when all we want to do is scream and judge and hate. If we refuse to turn the other cheek, if we're incapable of humbling ourselves and realizing that it could all too easily be us begging forgiveness and crying with regret and despair, then we can't expect to participate in the endeavor of life as a married person.

The hurdles that are presented to us throughout the course of married life are numerous and difficult to vault, but it is always possible. Whether you're dealing with infidelity, porn addiction, a dead bedroom, or emotional abuse, it is your outlook on yourself, on your life, on your spouse, and on the marriage you share together that will determine whether you're capable of working through it and moving on together with a better understanding of each other or check out as soon as things get hard. While no one can ever tell you when you should stay to try to make things work or when you should leave it all behind, I can tell you that no matter who you are married to, things will never be perfect. Making mistakes is a part of being human, and every marriage experiences its fair share of misgivings, missteps, and regret.

It is my sincere hope that with this book, everyone reading or listening to it may be able to better understand themselves and the circumstances and difficulties of their marriage. I've shown you what it takes to save your marriage by walking you through advice applicable both in general and in a set of specific circumstances; the rest is up to you to put into practice. I've tried to instill in you the knowledge that all these things boil down to is your willingness and ability to adapt and persevere. The rest is irrelevant.

Remember that marriage, for all of its difficulties and ordeals, is beautiful. Being successfully married is largely about being able to step back and look at the bigger picture to appreciate the wider context of the journey you're on together and just how lucky you are to have someone beside you who you can call your lover, best friend, and life partner, someone whom you can show forgiveness to and receive it in return, someone who you can love and hold in their worst moments and their best. Marriage is hard work, like anything that's worth doing in life. The trick is to go into it knowing it's going to be painful, knowing that it will hurt at times, but understanding that it will also be beautiful, full of light and love and laughter. Everybody hurts you sooner or later, and you hurt everybody in the exact same way. The trick is to find someone who you're willing to hurt for.

Book 2: Communication In Marriage

Discover The Secrets To Harnessing The Power Of Effective Communication In Your Marriage And Become A Better Spouse

Introduction

Marriage is a lot of hard work and doesn't always come easy or natural to some. Sharing everything in your life with another person takes a lot of dedication and compromise. Lack of and ineffective communication plays a key factor in many divorces. Many couples argue and fight, it can be extremely tiresome and frustrating. Perhaps you or your spouse continue to cry after an argument is seemingly already over. Or maybe something you argued about days ago comes back up because your spouse (or you) just couldn't, or wouldn't, let it go. Or perhaps you simply just do not know how to talk with each other without being emotional. Marriage is already difficult enough, learning how to effectively communicate with one another shouldn't be.

The vast majority of resolving marital issues

comes down to effective communication strategies. As simple as it sounds, being able to effectively communicate does not always come easy to many. It really doesn't matter what kind of communication problems that you struggle with, you can learn how to work on them and become a better communicator. Communication is a skill that can be learned and honed just like any other. Armed with the right knowledge, you can learn to effectively communicate with your spouse or significant other.

Whether you feel as though you are not being heard, that you don't ever seem to understand how your spouse is feeling or every time you try to talk with them about something it ends up turning into yelling and screaming, there is hope. In this book, I am going to show you a simple yet practical and proven methods for improving the communication not only with your spouse but in all relationships in your life. You will be able to quickly resolve and even prevent future arguments and come out of it being able to provide compassion and support to your loved ones while knowing the issue has been effectively resolved.

But first, who am I to give you advice on your marriage?

Hi, my name is Shirley Cole and I am a professional family therapist. Over the years I have worked with and coached hundreds of couples (and single people) on how to move out of relationship pain. I know this might seem like a strange profession, but I truly enjoy working with people and I love what I do. I am just so incredibly passionate about helping individuals and couples create healthy and meaningful relationships. Since 2004 I have been providing relationship counseling, as well as couples therapy, to people who have struggled in their love lives due to painful relationship patterns. Many of my clients, for years, had struggled to create respectful, loving, and life-affirming relationships before they began working with me.

Once you learn how to effectively communicate with your spouse, it can drastically change your relationship, for the better. Being able to have a conversation with your spouse without it ending in yelling or crying can feel like you are in a whole new relationship. You remember that feeling don't you? When everything your partner did made you laugh and smile and you would get those butterflies in your stomach whenever you got to see them. It doesn't matter if you have been married for a month or a few decades, learning how to communicate with your spouse helps you both feel heard and have the ability to resolve any issues the two of you might struggle with. We need to communicate in every area of your life, with our spouse, at our jobs, with our children, and with friends. Communicating with people is part of our everyday life, so why not hone that skill?

There are many reasons that couples split and get divorced. Communications problems and an inability to resolve conflicts are the two biggest causes of divorce.[1] We all have different ways of communicating and it should come as no surprise that men and women communicate differently. More often men find that nagging and complaining end their relationship, whereas women feel that their opinions are not validated. When someone feels as though they are not being heard or they are constantly being nagged at they will start to develop emotional walls that can be very difficult to break down. These emotional walls will only cause more issues and cause further communication barriers in your

---

[1] https://www.huffpost.com/entry/divorce-causes_n_4304466

relationship.

As humans we are creatures of habit, the things that happened in previous relationships and as we were children all help us to create habits in our lives now. Some of these habits can be good, like always saying "I love you," before going to bed, while some can be very bad, like resorting to name calling or physical aggression when you get angry. We all express our feelings in different ways. Some people avoid the issue, others use humor to try and cover up that they are hurting, while others will use anger and aggression. Learning how to communicate with your spouse is a major step in helping to break down your emotional walls.[2]

My coaching clients regularly praise me for changing their lives and helping them to develop deeper and more meaningful relationships with

---

[2] https://www.youtube.com/watch?v=oAeA3b_3CXQ

their significant other. In this book, I will reveal to you the necessary steps to effective communication in your relationship. This book will show you how anyone can enhance their relationship by learning how to communicate with less blame and more understanding of their partner.

In the event that you are having trouble communicating with your spouse or would just like to improve upon your communication skills in your relationships, this book is here to guide you! This book will help you to not only to express yourself to your spouse when you are feeling angry or overwhelmed, but it will also help you to effectively communicate everyday issues. You will learn how to adequately use positive language and how to understand each other's body language. Considering body language accounts for 55% of what we are actually saying, learning to decipher this can help immensely. Becoming a better communicator will also help you to become a better listener. Learning how to communicate also helps to cultivate trust and develop a healthy and lifelong relationship with your spouse.[3]

If you are arguing with your spouse on the regular, you are tearing away at the fabric of your relationship and eroding your marital foundation. Communication in marriage can break down quickly and cause a rippling effect in all other areas of your relationship. From your intimate life to parenting, to finances, once one area starts to break down, so do the others. Just as with a house, you need a strong foundation in order to make everything else work. You shouldn't have to go another day crying out of frustration and anger or yelling at one another simply because something was not communicated clearly. Both you and your spouse

---

[3] https://www.fulfillingyourvows.com/trust-in-your-marriage/

deserve the best possible relationship, and that starts with learning how to effectively communicate with one another and making sure each of you is heard loud and clear. Don't become just another statistic and wind up getting divorced simply because you can't express how you feel without turning into a crying fest or a knock down drag out fight.

Do you want to learn simple yet highly effective strategies to communicate with your spouse while building a strong, trusting relationship?

Couples are getting unnecessary divorce left and right all due to a lack of effective communication. They are fighting and breaking down their marital foundations all because they don't know how to express their feelings to one another without arguing. As a professional family therapist, I have seen it all.

If you are having problems communicating in your relationship and want to learn how to effectively work through them without having to resort to getting a divorce or never talking to each other, then you need this book! Don't put off learning better communication strategies "till tomorrow," start today! It takes time to work on your communication and learn how to express your feelings to one another while still validating each other.

In this book, I will show you how you can implement these communication strategies in your relationship today! Here is just a small portion of the strategies that I have packed into this book:

- How to understand body language and how to use it to improve your love life
- The secret on how to use positive communication (and what the heck positive

communication actually is!)
- The three most important tools in your communication toolbox
- How to get your point across and communicate through conflict and emotionally charged situations
- The keys to rebuilding trust when it has been lost
- How to repair your marriage when infidelity has occurred
- What destroys a marriage and how to bring it back from the brink
- How to keep love alive and how to handle when your spouse is driving you crazy
- And so much more!

Stop continuing to struggle in your marriage and take the reins to a better marriage. Even if you think your marriage is beyond repair you can take measures to fix it.

If you want to hone the communications skills that save your marriage and restore peace and harmony in your love life, then keep reading!

Chapter One:
Communicate Styles and What Our Bodies are Saying

We all communicate based on many factors including, our gender, the way we were raised, our personality types, all play a difference in how we communicate with other people. In this chapter, I will cover the difference in how men and women communicate. The secrets to using positive communication to increase your effectiveness in communicating with your spouse.[4] How you can understand body language to help you better understand your partner, and finally, the real reason to love and respect one another.

---

[4] https://www.youtube.com/watch?v=1b49ZmiLfoU

Differences in How Men and Women Communicate

You might not realize this but men and women speak different languages. Understanding the fundamentals of how men and women communicate will not only benefit you in your love life, it will also benefit you in any other relationship that you have.[5] At work, in school, in our family dynamics, we all communicate with the opposite sex. When men and women do not communicate in each other's language it can cause a perfect storm of emotions and ineffective communication.[6] This can then cause confusion, drama, disappointment, unrealized expectations, hurt feelings, anger, and many other avoidable problems. Learning how to effectively communicate with the opposite sex will help to

---

[5] http://blog.loopline-systems.com/en/the-differences-between-male-and-female-communication-style-in-workplace

[6] https://www.enkirelations.com/differences-between-male-and-female-communication.html

make all of your relationships easier with the ability to effortlessly communicate resulting in fulfilling and drama-free relationships.

When we understand that we are different and that our core needs are different, we can work to radically transform our marriage. A woman wants to prevent issues in the marriage by talking about issues regularly, while a man might not think there are issues until they talk about them on a regular basis.

While not every man and every woman communicate in the same way. Some men might have similar communication styles to women and some women might have similar communication styles to men. Women communicate a certain way and men communicate in a different way, however, they are not mutually exclusive. Let's first take a look at the core of the communication styles of women.

How women communicate

Women communicate from a place of emotion. Communication is used to release negative feelings and create a stronger bond with her partner. To express her thoughts, concepts, feelings, emotions, and ideas, she will use relational examples to communicate. Although she might not realize it, she can often solve her problems and issues just by talking aloud about them to her partner. The goal of this is to help her organize her thoughts and feelings that she is carrying around. All sides of the situation need to be explored and determined if there are any other options that will help to solve her problem and to gain some perspective. She just wants to feel she is being heard in a supportive and non-judgmental way. She isn't necessarily looking for the man to provide her with a solution. Women also seek to increase intimacy in a relationship through communication with their partner. When a woman feels that she is being listened to, it helps to ease her anxieties and reduces her negative feelings.

Women seldom hesitate to ask advice or seek help from a man. She seeks to improve upon her situation but also does not want to feel like an unnecessary burden to the man. It is in her evolutionary DNA that women should rely on men to help them solve their problems.

When a conflict arises, women use communication to process their thoughts and emotions to help eliminate their negative feelings. Women seek to be asked compassionate questions and someone who will listen as she works through exploring her thoughts and feelings. This often might require talking through her issues with a girlfriend or other female counterpart as she knows that she will be able to get her emotional needs met when communicating with another woman.

In order to effectively communicate with her male counterparts, she should tell men exactly what they need them to do. In a romantic relationship, speaking in plain terms about what she wants her man to do will help her feel loved and validated. Women should avoid speaking in relational examples while expecting men to figure out what point they are trying to make and where they are coming from. Women need to tell men in steps what they expect from them. Below is an example of how a woman can communicate to a man that she has an issue and would like to talk about it to him so he can make her feel validated and loved.

A woman sends an email/text to her male partner about a job interview she has where she mentioned that it did not turn out well. Instead of expecting him to ask about it later on when they get together, she should specifically state that she wants to discuss the situation and get her frustrations off of her chest.

"Honey, you know that job interview I had today. It DID NOT go as planned. I am feeling very emotional about the situation and would like to talk about it right away with you when I see you later. I just need to vent, I don't want you to try and fix it. Please ask me about it right away when you get home!"

This message outlines to the male partner how she is feeling and what she wants him to do. She just wants him to ask about the situation and then listen to how she feels about it. An ineffective communication to the man would look like this:

"I had a terrible day, job interview went horrible, I can't wait to see you later!"

All this is saying to the man is that her day did not go well. He will not know to ask her about the job interview or that he just needs to listen to her so she will feel validated and loved. Just because the woman mentioned something to the man earlier about the job interview, she should not expect him to immediately ask her about it when he sees her. This is an unreasonable expectation. Although women might think otherwise, men cannot read their minds and vice versa. Then when a woman has an expectation that is not met they often become angry and she feels like her partner doesn't care about her. Women should never assume that a man knows what they want, she needs to lay it out for the man.

How men communicate

Men use reason and logic to communicate and relate to situations and relationships. They are always trying to be the problem solvers and fix things for their significant other. Communication for them is direct and efficient, less chit chat. They only share details essential to the conversation. Whereas, most of the time women would just prefer them to listen. One of the best things a man can do in order to effectively communicate with his woman is to simply ask them what they want. Should men give their opinion and try and fix the situation or does your partner just need you to listen? Men want to feel successful in making his woman feel happy. When a man feels he has been unsuccessful in making his woman feel happy he withdraws and leave either physically or emotionally.

It is a very well known statistic that men have sex on their mind most of the time. When a woman is upset about something the man can come across as being insensitive about her needs if he is making sexual advances towards her. This is another very common form of miscommunication. Even though a woman might not be turning down the man's sexual advances, she is just upset and wants to get something off of her chest, the man will feel that he is being turned down and thus sexually rejected. This will only cause further frustration and a breakdown in communication. The man will then feel unsuccessful as he cannot make his woman happy and feels like a failure.

Often when a woman starts the conversation, the man will feel as though she is seeking advice from him. This will turn on his problem-solving detectors and he will then listen and try to identify her issues and immediately want to offer a solution to that problem. Men will then often feel the need to interrupt a woman when she is speaking to offer advice, which will make her feel angry. Men might also feel that if a woman is coming to them to vent about something that they are the problem. This can lead to feelings of inadequacy and make them become defensive. Being able to patiently listen is not a skill that men inherently have.

When a man is experiencing conflict, he simply wants to forget about his problems to reduce his stress. He will try and focus on other things like watching television, playing video games or fixing a car. Something that doesn't require him to think about his issues and get his mind focused on something else. In extreme cases, he might even turn to forms of self-medication, such as drinking, to forget about his issues. When a woman then tries to comfort him, this can lead to further withdrawing. The best way to handle communication with a man when conflict arises is to let him work things out on his own. When he is ready he will come and talk to you about what is wrong. Sitting there and consistently poking at him will lead to further aggravation and withdraw.

Let's refer back to the message that was sent earlier that was poorly communicated to the man to see how he might respond to it without being told exactly what to do.

"I had a terrible day, job interview went horrible, I can't wait to see you later!"

He might not realize that she will want to talk

about her terrible day and how the job interview went. He will see "I can't wait to see you later," and think about the things he wants to tell her or become excited because they might engage in sexual activity later. Thus upon seeing her later, he doesn't ask about her day or the job interview and makes sexual advances toward her. She becomes upset, he becomes upset, and an argument ensues. He cannot read her mind and know that she needed to just talk to him and that he just needed to listen. Even if your spouse is not great at communicating, you can work on things to better understand what they are trying to say.

There is a more effective way that the man could have communicated in response to the woman's message upon meeting that would have met both of their needs. He could have asked her if she wanted to talk about her day and the job interview upon seeing her and let her communicate her feelings. He could have said something like:

"Hi honey, it sounds like you had a bad day and your job interview didn't go well, tell me about it. I'm here to listen."

Even if a man asks her if she wants to talk, things can get tricky. Perhaps she wants to talk about her issues but is having difficulty communicating and expressing her feelings on the matter. Here, if he were to ask her "do you want to talk about it," he is presenting her with a close-ended question. Therefore she may respond with a "no" even though she does want to talk about it. When you use open-ended questions in your language, you force the person you are talking with to think about their answer.

So what are the typical differences in

communication styles of men and women?[7]

- Women are more likely to talk with other women about their problems or when they need to decide something.
- Women seek relationships with other women based on interests and find common ways to connect with one another.
- Women focus on building rapport and building bonds with one another by sharing their experiences and asking questions.
- When women have a disagreement with each other it will affect all aspects of their relationship.
- Men like to keep their problems to themselves and don't see why they should share their problems with others.
- Men relate to one another based on a power dynamic with status and dominance being important factors.

---

[7] https://www.youtube.com/watch?v=Dugka_UssTM

- Men share experiences competitively and like to tell information rather than asking questions.
- When men have a disagreement they move on to another subject and still interact with one another.

We are constantly having an internal battle with our civilized perspective of communication and our evolutionary biology. Thus we should not blame or criticize the other gender for how they communicate but seek to understand and learn to adapt our own communication styles. We can do this by learning about and implementing positive communication.

All communication requires a sender and a receiver, this is the basic model of all communication. The message originates with the sender and sent to the receiver. Before the sender can send the message, it needs to be encoded into some language or code. Before the receiver can receive the message it must be decoded. Where it gets complicated is the sender assumes the receiver already knows the code. To complicate it even further, between the coding and decoding the message must also pass through the noise. This can be physical noise, like a child crying, or mental noise, such as, thinking about what to make for dinner when your partner is trying to communicate with you. Noise can also mean history, experiences, or gender. What happens then is the original message that the sender is trying to send gets jumbled up and not received to the receiver clearly. There are things that you can do to make sure that the message that is sent and received is the same message.

Here are five things that you can do to encourage positive communication:[8]

---

[8] https://www.youtube.com/watch?v=PF1ACxdiDow

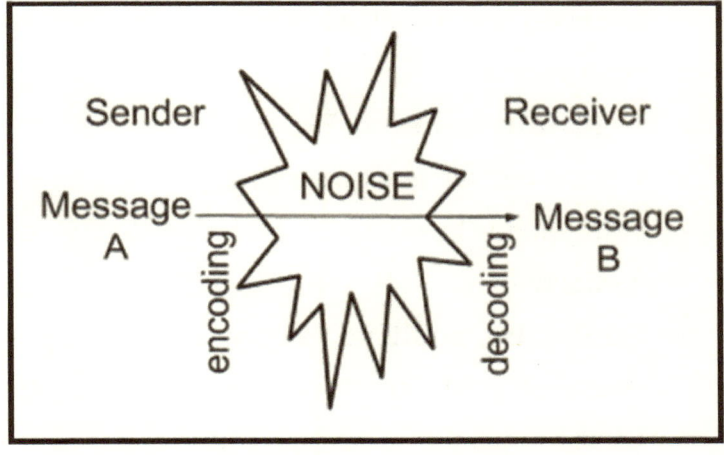

1. **Listen.** Listen more than you speak. Listen to understand and reflect what you are hearing. For example, *"it sounds like you are saying..."*
2. **Seek to understand, not just to agree.** Understanding the message and agreeing with it is not the same thing! Often people feel that if they show the sender that they understand that they will also feel that they are agreeing with them. This is not always the case.
3. **Stay focused on your audience.** Try to

focus on how other people are feeling rather than yourself.
4. **Maintain contact.** Eye contact is just one form. Your facial expressions, your gestures, your body language, are also forms of contact.
5. **Smile, be positive, say yes!** Saying yes does not mean that you are agreeing with what the person is saying. You are, however, communicating that you are actively listening to them and hearing their message. This helps to create positive energy in the communication to help get the correct message across.

When you work on implementing these five tactics, you can encourage positive communication while also learning to effectively communicate.

Think about this for a minute, with all of the

things that can go wrong with communication (see the diagram above) it is amazing that anyone can communicate effectively. Many times in a relationship the sender and receiver are getting different messages. The husband says something to the wife and the wife replies back with "*so you think...*" and it is NOT the message that the husband had originally sent. It may have been an issue with encoding, or decoding, or the noise in between but whatever the issue was, the message did not come across as it was originally sent.

There are a few things that you can do in your communication so that what is sent is exactly the same thing that is received.

First of all, silent the noise in your mind, be present and listen to understand your partner. Don't try and think of your answer or the input you want to give while the other person is talking. More often than not, couples do not disagree as much as they think they do. They are not listening to understand the other person.

Second, express to be understood. The goal is the same in both situations, understanding. You don't want to express to persuade, convince, manipulate, or to bring the other person into our point of view. This means that you need to pay attention to your language, not just what you are saying, but how you are saying it, what your body language is saying and what your facial expressions are saying.[9] Do your best to encode your message so it will be accurately received and decoded.

Just as with any other skill, practice will make you better. Practice what words you say, how you say them, and your body language.

---

[9] https://www.psychologytoday.com/us/blog/beyond-words/201109/is-nonverbal-communication-numbers-game

Body language can be a powerful tool but unfortunately, people often stereotype what body language means and how it can help them effectively communicate. Body language is just one of three aspects of how we communicate. There are the words we speak, the tone in which we speak them, and our gestures and body language.

In a conversation, conflict can arise more often from the tone of our voice rather than from the words we are actually saying.[10] Your tone of voice and your body language and gestures hold more weight in a conversation than what you are actually saying. If you are portraying a mixed message, the person you are speaking to will actually discount your words and believe what your tone and body are saying.

---

[10] https://thesystemsthinker.com/communicating-through-conflict/

Learning how to communicate more effectively can help you to reach other goals in your life as well. You should not only be aware of how to read body language in others but also how to effectively communicate your message with your non-verbal cues.[11] One way to practice reading people's body language is to give people compliments. Many times people will react as though they are physically pushing the compliment away. Our brains are unable to distinguish pushing away something that is bad and something good. So by default, we can inadvertently push away a lot of good things.

Body language is a skill that can also be honed. We all have certain automatic reactions to things but with body language, we can learn to control and use it in certain ways. Changing your body language can also create a psychological change. If we enhance our body language it can also

---

[11] https://www.youtube.com/watch?v=nT6pqlUutlU

enhance our psychological programming. This can also lead to liking yourself more and other people like you as well.

Going back to giving and receiving compliments. Here is a simple exercise to start with: when someone gives you a compliment, act as if you are scooping it up and placing it in your heart and say *"thank you,"* in a positive and sincere tone.

There is an aspect of body language that both men and women do but it means two completely different things. When a woman nods her head during a conversation, it is to show that they are listening. This then signals to the man (in his mind) that she is agreeing with him. He then makes the assumption that the woman agrees with him and will go along with his idea. The woman has no idea that he has converted this information and will later have no idea why the man thought she agreed with his statement or idea since he never directly asked her or specifically said that she agreed with him.

When a man nods his head he is showing that he agrees with the statement or idea. When a woman is speaking to a man and he does not nod his head, she will then assume that he either disagrees with her or is not listening to her.

We often create physical barriers when we are in conversation with your significant others - These include closing your hands in front of you, such as crossing your arms, you are creating what is called a gate. This signifies that you are feeling less than or that you feel weak. This can also be a self-protective mechanism. Placing your hands at your sides in a relaxed manner opens you up. It will feel very awkward at first, but over time it is one more body language skill you can perfect. Now you can certainly still "talk" with your hands as many people do, but then when you are done using them, place them back at your sides. When you stand in a stance that portrays confidence it helps to feed your subconscious with feelings of confidence and create a whole new energy.

Before you can focus on learning what other people's body language means, you first need to learn how to focus on your own body language. Unfortunately, in today's society, people are often too busy looking at their phones and unable to use body language to communicate effectively. We need to be taught how to communicate with body language just like any other language because we are not watching it and paying attention to it all the time.

When you see someone doing something with their body language, try it on. This means that when you see someone communicate some body language that seems confusing to you, such as rubbing their arm in the middle of a conversation, do it yourself later on while communicating with a different person. You don't want to mirror what the person is doing back to them or try and confront them about why they used that particular body language or judge them. Then when you try on that body language, later on, ask yourself:

- What does that feel like?
- Why would I use that same body language?

This will then start a whole new thought process that might help shed some light on what that body language means to that person. This is a great way to let your body teach you what different types of body language might mean. While each different move and touch has some kind of meaning to it, you don't specifically need to know all the idiosyncrasies to understand what someone else is trying to say with their body.

When people feel they are being understood it increases connection and builds rapport. For example, when you are in a conversation with someone and they turn one of their feet away from you, this often means that they are ready to be done with the conversation. If you understand this, you can then recognize that that person is done with the conversation and quickly wrap it up. This helps them to feel understood, which is one of the most powerful uses of body language. When you understand what people are saying with their body language you become both a better listener and a better communicator.

There is a lot of information you can get from a person just by understanding the body language, specifically from their eyes. When you are speaking with someone and you ask them a question, you can generally tell what kind of answer they are going to give you just by what direction their eyes go in. There are four different directions that someone will look before answering a question and this can give you some big clues as to what kind of answer they are going to give you. Your eye movement also helps to trigger a memory.

If someone looks up to their left before giving you an answer to a question, they are looking into the left side of their brain. The left side of the brain is the analytical side that provides you with an answer that is related to data, numbers, facts, and past things. When someone looks up and to their right, they are looking into the right side of their brain. This will be an answer that is a big picture, imagination, creativity, or future things.

When someone looks straight to either side, they are listening to something that someone has told them or something that they have read. When someone looks straight down before answering, their answer will be based on emotion. The longer they look down the more emotional it will be. Knowing what kind of answer they are going to give you can help you communicate with them better and build rapport. For example, if someone looks down before giving you your answer, don't try and pull them up too quickly or steer them towards giving you an answer that is not emotional.[12] Be patient and let them process their answer and don't try and divert the conversation by asking another question or telling a joke. You don't need to try and rescue the person, let them feel what they are feeling and let them give you their answer.

Once you have become fluent in body language you will be able to easily detect when things don't align. When you see that body language doesn't match with the words they are saying, it is time to ask more questions. You are not trying to interrogate the person, just trying to figure out what they are actually trying to say. Just as with verbal communication, you are seeking to understand. When you are able to let someone feel what they are feeling, you are able to learn from them and show that person respect for their

---

[12] https://www.psychologytoday.com/us/blog/fulfillment-any-age/201412/4-ways-improve-your-emotional-communication

feelings and build a connection with them. One of the keys to understanding body language is to not judge based on what you see.[13]

So the three keys to reading body language are:

- Leave out the judgment
- Try on the body language of others
- When the words and the body language don't match, ask more questions

---

[13] https://www.youtube.com/watch?v=9aWFOK46eqA

The Differences Between Love and Respect and the Reason for Each

Love and respect, these are two emotions we just can't get enough of![14]

While we all have a general idea of what love is, it can be hard to define as there are many forms of it. It is not a concrete concept but rather a subjective one. Love, true love (as in a relationship) can be characterized by a triangle of traits; intimacy, passion, and commitment.

Intimacy is often confused with romantic love, while they can exist in the same relationship, they are not exclusive to one another. Intimacy can take place in friendship, between family members, and of course, in romantic

---

[14] https://www.focusonthefamily.com/marriage/communication-and-conflict/6-tools-for-healthy-communication-in-marriage

relationships.[15] It focuses on a deep connection that you share with another person. This can happen quickly when you find someone who shares many of your traits and interests and you "hit it off" with them well. This can happen in both friendships and relationships. While a romantic relationship does not need to be present for intimacy to take place, it is not likely that a healthy romantic relationship will develop if there is a lack of intimacy.

Passion is solely for romantic partnerships where there is a sexual attraction to someone. It is difficult for a romantic relationship to flourish, or to be maintained over long periods of time, without passion. While you can certainly have passion without intimacy, a healthy romantic relationship contains both. Passion can take place in love or just in lust with one another.

---

[15] https://www.familylife.com/podcast/familylife-today/the-real-reason-to-love-and-respect/

While passion can certainly fade over time in a long-standing relationship, a healthy one will maintain it to some degree.

In a healthy romantic relationship, each person is committed to one another and are willing to work to build and maintain their future together. If a couple can not commit to one another, it is likely that the relationship won't last very long. Commitment does not necessarily mean marriage in this case. There are many unmarried couples that have committed to one another and are thriving. While you can certainly have a relationship with the commitment that lacks passion and intimacy, a strong, healthy, and long-lasting relationship will have similarly equal parts of all three components.

We often view respect in connection with our culture. It contains both how we verbally communicate with someone and the body language we use, such as shaking someone's hand and looking them in the eye when you greet them. You should be respectful of those around you, whether they are strangers or committed lovers. Respect is treating someone in a positive manner because of their relationship with you. This might be a total stranger or a loved one. We generally respect people of authority and those that have somehow earned respect from us in one way or another. While everyone has their own viewpoints on who should be respected and why it is ultimately your decision. Perhaps you distrust your local government, thus are not respectful of them. While some people might think that their parents should always be respected, others might feel it depends on their past and present actions.

The biggest difference between respect and love is that respect is meant to be shown to everyone while love is only shown to a select few. Everyone should, at least initially, deserve your respect. It can be difficult to earn respect from others if you do not show anyone respect, to begin with. Avoid disrespecting people unless you have a valid reason to. Even then, showing respect when someone else is being disrespectful makes you the bigger person in that situation.

Relationships require both love and respect to work. You should be able to love and respect each other as a person, as lovers, and your individual opinions and choices (within reason of course). There are certain aspects of your relationship that you should respect, such as boundaries, accomplishments, each other's wishes, and friends and family.

Respecting each other's boundaries can include anything from giving each other space in the bathroom or during an argument. Even though you love each other and might want to spend all of your time together, you still need to maintain boundaries both physically and emotionally. This also gives you the opportunity to have a little bit of "me" time and still remain individual people.

I'm sure this has happened at some point in your life. You did something you are very proud of, and the person you can't wait to tell about it the most just does not share in your enthusiasm. That can be very disheartening and maybe even make you not want to share accomplishments in the future. If you are working on reaching a goal together, try and encourage one another and respect the goal and the process.

This can be extremely difficult if you don't particularly like each other's friends and family. The key here is that you don't necessarily need to like them, you just need to show them respect. When you enter into a relationship with someone, you are also entering into [some kind] of relationship with their friends and family. Don't make any disagreements worse by disrespecting them.

Respecting each other's wishes goes hand in hand with the boundaries that we discussed earlier. While boundaries might be implied, respecting your partner's wishes is based on something they have asked you to do or not to do. For example, if one partner smokes and the other does not, perhaps they have expressed that they don't like the partner smoking in the house, so they go outside. This is respecting their wishes.

While these ideas are not mutually exclusive to men or women, gender generally plays a role in love and respect in a marriage. There is still a very archaic thought process when it comes to love and respect within a marriage based on gender role.[16] The man is supposed to show the woman love and shower her with affection. While the woman is supposed to show the man respect and take care of his needs. While this worked well for many people for many years, in a perfect relationship, love and respect are mutual rather than roughed in gender norms. Men also want to feel loved and women also want to feel respected. Neither love nor respect is more or less important in a relationship, respect is like the glue that holds together intimacy, passion, and commitment. While we might like to think that love is all you need in a strong relationship, that is simply not the case. It is a melting pot of intimate love, passionate love, committed love, and respect that will help a relationship to withstand even the toughest patches.

---

[16] https://www.regain.us/advice/love/what-is-the-difference-between-love-and-respect/

Chapter Summary

Since the dawn of time, men and women have communicated differently. We can use the same words, have the same tone, and use the same body language but the message we are trying to deliver and the message that gets received are generally two completely different things. Understanding the different fundamentals of how men and women communicate will not only benefit you in your love life but in every other relationship in your life.

Generally speaking women communication from a place of emotion and use this to release negative feelings and to create a stronger bond with her partner. Women often can solve most of their issues simply by talking about them and do not seek advice from a man when she is expressing her thoughts and feelings about a situation. Women also use communication as a means to increase intimacy with their partner. When she feels that she is being listened to this helps to reduce her anxieties and negative feelings.

On the other hand, men communicate use reason and logic. They don't care about chit chat and want to be the problem solvers and fix their partner's situation then they think something is wrong. Men thrive on feeling successful in making women feel happy. When he is unsuccessful he reacts by withdrawing from her or the situation.

For a woman to effectively communicate with a man, she should tell him exactly what she needs, wants, and expects. Communicate to him in a logical and step by step format without using relational examples. If a woman wants to vent to her man about something, she should specifically state that, not expect him to read her mind.

When a woman starts to express herself to a man this will turn on his problem-solving detectors and he will immediately start to look for an issue that he can solve. In order for a man to effectively listen to a woman, he needs to actually listen to what she is saying then repeat it back to her in his own words and ask if that is what she was trying to communicate. This signals to the woman that he is listening and makes her feel validated.

When men experience some type of conflict, he simply wants to forget about it and move on. In order to do this he will focus on other things to get his mind off of the issue, such as watching television. The best way for a woman to handle conflict with a man is to let him work it out on his own. If left alone he should eventually come around. Constantly asking him what is wrong will only cause aggravation.

Below are some key points in how men and women can communicate effectively to one another:

- Women communicate with emotions to express feelings and work through issues.
- Men communicate using direct messages while using reason and logic.
- Women should be allowed to vent without men trying to fix their problems.
- Men should listen to women and repeat back what they heard in their own words.
- Women should specifically communicate to men what they want.
- Men should ask open-ended questions to women.

We must seek to understand one another's communication styles and adapt our own communication styles. Implementing positive communication can drastically help cut through the gender differences and make sure that the message that is getting sent and the message that is received is the same. There are five main things that you can do in order to encourage positive communication:

1. Listen.
2. Seek to understand, not just to agree.
3. Stay focused on your audience.
4. Maintain appropriate eye contact.
5. Smile, be positive, and say yes!

Effective communication is a skill that can be learned just like any other. Here are some quick tips when it comes to effectively sending and receiving messages to make sure they are the same thing:

- Silent the noise.
- Seek to understand.
- Seek to be understood.

You need to remain conscious about not only the words you are saying, your tone of voice, and your body language. Effectively communicating in all of these areas carries over to other aspects of your life, including work and parenting. Nodding in a conversation means two completely different things to men and women. To men it means agreement, to women is signifies listening. Closed hands in front of you in any way is a signal of being closed off or is self-protective. Learn to pay attention to your own and other people's body language.

The direction that someone's eyes look when you ask them questions can give you specific clues to what type of response you will receive.

- Up and to the left = an analytical answer or related to the past
- Up and to the right = a creative answer of related to the future

- Straight to either side = recalling something they heard or read
- Straight down = an emotional answer

The key here is to understand and not to judge people for their body language.

True love is a subjective concept characterized by intimacy, passion, and commitment. Intimacy is the deep connection that you share with another person and is not related to a significant other. Passion is solely meant for a romantic relationship and related to sexual attraction. Commitment refers to the willingness to work things out and build your future together. Love should only be given to your partner, while respect should be given to all the people you encounter.

In a committed and loving relationship, respect each other's boundaries and wishes, accomplishments, and each other's friends and family. You need all of it to thrive in a healthy relationship, intimate love, committed love, passionate love, and respect.

In the next chapter, you will learn how to build up your communications toolbox.

Chapter Two: Building Your Communication Toolbox

Becoming a better communicator all starts with becoming a better listener. Hearing what someone is saying is not the same as listening to what they are saying. When you listen you are hearing the words they are saying, understanding their body language and their tone of voice, then decoding that message. In this chapter, we are going to cover how to listen effectively, the important tools to communicate better, how to communicate through conflict, and how you can communicate through difficult emotions.

In chapter one we covered how message A can turn into message B if the encoding and decoding don't line up, or there is too much noise it can create problems. Your goal when listening shouldn't be to offer advice or to solve someone's problem, it should simply be to understand. Understand how they are feeling and what they are trying to say. If you are the sender of the message, you should also express to be understood. You are not saying that you are agreeing when you understand someone, you are simply seeking to understand their point of view and expressing to be understood.

There are a few ways that you can use indicators to signal that you are listening and understanding the other person. Using the reflective listening technique is one way to help the person you are communicating with to let them know that you are seeking to understand and actually listening to them.[17] This can be done by simply repeating back to them what you heard in your own words what they said. *"Ok, so what you are saying is..."* You should then be able to immediately tell if you are on the right track. If you see the lights go on and they are agreeing with you, then you know you are doing your job. However, if they show any form of hesitation, you didn't get it, you haven't hit the nail on the head just yet.

---

[17] https://hbr.org/2017/12/how-to-control-your-emotions-during-a-difficult-conversation

Reflective listening is a skill that you can learn that will help you become a very effective listener. This will help to ensure that message A equals message A and the person you are communicating with knows that they are being understood.

There are three very important and simple tools that you can use to communicate better in your marriage (and just about every other relationship in your life). There are many tools that you can include in your communication toolbox.[18] Don't feel like you have to implement all of these things all at once. Try and focus on one or two at a time and work those skills into your daily life.

Have you ever had someone ask you something (maybe a child) and the timing was terrible? This can carry over into communications with your spouse as well. If you carefully choose the timing

---

[18] https://www.imom.com/3-communication-tools-your-marriage-needs/

of your conversation with your spouse, you will likely have greater success. It is difficult to try and have a serious conversation when the kids are running around screaming, or one of you has just gotten home from work after a terrible day. If you want your spouse to truly hear you and listen to what you are saying, timing is a key factor. This can be for a more difficult conversation or even one where you just want your significant other to share in your excitement.

If you are questioning whether or not you should talk to your spouse about something at that point in time, think of the word HALT.[19] This stands for **H**ungry, **A**ngry, **L**onely, and **T**ired. If either of you is experiencing any of these, hold off on having that conversation. While it is ideal to have serious conversations when the timing is right,

---

[19] https://www.familylife.com/articles/topics/marriage/staying-married/communication/5-communication-tools-that-saved-my-marriage/

that is not always possible. Sometimes you have to have a conversation right then and there. If this happens, do your best, as a couple to minimize distractions and hold your conversation.

It can be easy to lash out at someone when you are both angry, which can then perpetuate the argument even further. Responding to your spouse instead of reacting gives the person who is responding to the power to end the argument. Married couples (or any couple for that matter) often have arguments that start out of a lack of communication. When an argument has started because of a lack of communication, you have the power to stop it in its tracks. You might think the person who has started the argument is the one that has the most power to stop it, this is not true. The person who has the most control to stop the argument is the one who responds to it rather than reacts to it. Instead of reacting, or overreacting, to an argument that has started, respond to it to stop the argument. Approach this in a neutral tone and don't get defensive or place blame.

We discussed earlier the noise that people can experience while encoding and decoding a message. This can be external noise, like the TV being on, or internal noise, like thinking about something we want to talk about and not actually listening to your partner. Have you ever driven in a really bad storm? How focused were you on the road and making sure you could see the white lines? I bet you didn't have the music blaring or were scrolling through your phone. Think about this the next time you and your spouse are talking, it doesn't have to be a serious conversation, it can be about everyday things. This can actually be the best time to practice this tool so that way when you do get into a more serious discussion you will have some experience in tuning out the noise and being focused. When you are talking to your spouse, use direct eye contact. Try and turn off any external noise possible. Instead of waiting for your spouse to bring it up, initiate a conversation about your spouse's concerns.

We can not read one another's minds. The way we look at an issue through our lens of thought and reasoning is not the same as how our partner sees the same issue through their lens. This can cause many arguments and issues as we tend to ignore each other's unique perspectives. Do your best to clarify EXACTLY what you mean from the beginning of your conversation. For example, if your spouse asks you to grab something from the store on the way home from work, ask them specifically about what they want. This should help to eliminate any expected mind reading.

I have already talked about seeking to understand when you listen to your spouse. This is where questioning comes in. Don't simply ask them questions as if you are interrogating them. Ask them questions in a neutral and caring tone that lets them know you are trying to fully understand what they are saying. Instead of worrying about how you are going to reply to what it is they said or offer your input, just listen. Then ask them another question to show them that you were listening and are seeking to understand what they are saying. Think of it like this... *"so I am hearing you say [this], how does that make you feel?"* Or something of that nature.

Many people do not understand the benefits of using technology in their communication as it is often seen as a barrier. If you allow it, technology can be a huge distraction, looking at your phone while your partner is trying to have a conversation with you, or continuing to look at the TV for the score of the game. The person who is trying to talk to you is going to feel like you are not listening to them. When your spouse is trying to talk to you, step away from the technology and give them your full attention. If you go out with each other, leave your phones in the car. Remove your television from your bedroom and make it a technology-free zone. Technology can also be used for good in a relationship. When you are away from each other, send short and fun messages to one another.

A habit is something that you do consistently, often without thinking about it. It takes about 28 days to make something into a habit. You can create a simple habit tracker using a calendar and put an X on each day that you are doing something to create that habit. A few things that you can work on creating habits with your spouse include saying *"I love you,"* connecting with them while you are away from each other, and praying together.

When you first begin dating, you find all the things about your partner that you love and find cute. From the way they tie their shoes to the way, they eat their cereal. It is easy to see these things when the relationship is new and exciting, it is not so easy to see the wonder in someone when you are knee deep in kids, bills, and other stressors. Try to look for these things intentionally, try and keep a small journal for a month where every day you write down things you are grateful for about your spouse. Then, at the end of the month, show it to them. This not only shows them that you still find them amazing in so many ways but that you still see them. When you are in conflict with one another, always try and reaffirm the strength of your relationship[20] with something like, *"I'm very upset with you right now, that doesn't mean I don't love and adore you, I just need to take a minute to cool down."*

While it's easy to snuggle up with one another when you are feeling affectionate, it can be difficult to engage in positive physical touch when you are arguing with one another. Positive touch includes anything from holding hands, to having your legs crossed one another, whatever you and your spouse are comfortable with. If you know you are sitting down to talk about something that could have some tension, engage in positive touch with one another. This serves two purposes. When we are lovingly touching each other, there is less likely of a chance that an argument will ensue. If it does and there is a physical separation this is a clear body language sign that the discussion has taken a turn.

---

[20] https://www.focusonthefamily.com/marriage/communication-and-conflict/the-walls-in-your-marriage

It can be very easy to hear what someone says but not really listen to them. When you mirror your spouse, you can help to easily eliminate misunderstandings. This is a very simple tool that you can use with your spouse and anyone else you are communicating within your life. When you are engaged in a conversation, repeat back what you heard that person say in your own words. *"What I'm hearing you say is..."* You can also try and mirror their body language. If they are leaning back in the chair when you are talking to them, you can also lean back in a chair. The point of mirroring in a conversation is not to defend your point or tear down the other person, the point is to seek to fully understand what they are saying and meaning.

Lastly, you can use the STOP tool as an effective way to help control a conversation that might be getting out of control. This consists of stop, time out, own your own part, and peace offering. The first thing you need to do is stop! If the conversation is going in a way that feels uncomfortable, stop the conversation. Next, take a timeout from one another. This could be thirty minutes to an hour of physical space away from each other, or even longer if needed, to cool down and regain your composure. The next step is to own your own part. This is not the time to defend your position or attach your partner, this is the time to think about and discuss your role in the miscommunication. Lastly, you want to come back to one another with a peace offering. This should be something positive, such as a promise to change a behavior or to give your partner some kind of positive affirmation.

Learning to communicate with each other in marriage can be difficult. Especially, newly married couples who may have difficulty figuring out what the other spouse is saying. It can also be very difficult to effectively communicate through conflict and emotion but there are things that you can do to help.[21]

If you have ever been in a heated argument with someone you know how difficult it can be to try and effectively get your message across. Either what you are trying to say isn't coming out the way you want, or the person you are talking to isn't hearing you correctly. When we are hurt or feeling unheard, we can often resort to criticism. When you criticize someone you often attack their character, personality, or sense of self. Criticism often takes something that happened during a specific situation and turns it into a personality flaw by using words like, *"never,"* and *"always."* Things like, *"you are always so busy with [thing], you never care about what I am doing!"* When you continually criticize one another, that can turn into contempt for each other. This can lead to patterns of cruel jokes,

---

[21] https://www.psychologytoday.com/intl/blog/counseling-keys/201704/communicating-through-conflict

sarcastic disdain, and a general meanness and disrespect for one another. This will only serve to erode the relationship even further.

Criticizing our partner often has nothing to do with them, it has to do with how you feel. This harmful tactic can arise when you feel as though you haven't been heard or understood. Criticizing your partner is a way to make yourself heard, a way of feeling that it will help to get your partner's attention. What most people don't realize is that it often has the complete opposite effect. If you do this you are sabotaging your communication. When we perceive that we are being attacked our defensive mechanism kicks in and we prepare to fight back, which then turns our effective listening receptors off. Criticism often creates a cycle of conflict and blaming and inhibit positive and productive communication.

When we engage in a conflict or perceive that

there is a conflict about to arise, our primal instincts often kick in and the flight, fight, or freeze response takes over.[22] When you feel that there is a conflict arising, do you automatically feel the need to fight back? Do you just give up and leave? Or do you shut down, withdraw, and become emotionally numb? None of these scenarios are necessarily bad or good, it is just how our brains were conditioned to react. When our brains have been emotionally hijacked by our evolutionary instincts, you can't process using our frontal lobe, which its main purpose is to problem solve and make decisions.

Instead of approaching things from an either/or perspective, you can work to approach issues from a both/and perspective. Using a both/and perspective allows you to see both sides of the coin, so to speak. Use empathy in your statements and let the other person know that

---

[22] https://www.psychologytoday.com/intl/blog/the-connected-life/201706/five-keys-good-communication-during-conflict

you understand how they are feeling, even if you don't agree with them. You can disagree with someone without it feeling personal or like an attack. Being able to approach things from a both/and perspective will help to build trust, ensure safety, and increase connection which will then lead to overall better communication and decision making.

There are several strategies that you can use in order to foster effective communication while in conflict (or if you feel conflict is about to arise).

When we become upset we often react emotionally. There are two issues with this, the reaction and the emotion. While this is understandable, try to approach the matter in a calm and collected fashion. If you are upset about something and need to approach your partner, try taking a few deep breaths and think about some of their good qualities (not that they have to be constantly reminded to empty the dishwasher). This will help to put you in a more positive frame of mind rather than one of blame and anger.

This might be the one you have heard of before as it is a classic counseling technique. This helps you to clearly express how you are feeling without your partner feeling as though you are blaming them. Start your statement to your partner with *"I feel,"* rather than *"you..."* This lets your partner know that you are focusing on how you feel about the situation rather than your partner's flaws. Instead of saying, *"you always forget to take out the garbage,"* try *"I feel hurt and like I am not being heard when you forget to take the garbage out."* This can dramatically change the way your partner reacts to you.

While it might be easy to bring something up that happened last year to try and reiterate your point, it is not going to lead to more effective communication. When you are in a discussion or argument, talk about that specific incident rather than focusing on past experiences or arguments. Using words like *"always"* and *"never,"* lead to categorizing your partner with global character flaws. Keep your conversation specific to what is currently happening and don't try and support your claim or point of view by bringing up past incidents. By focusing on the specific issue at hand you can minimize the intensity of the argument.

When we get into an argument we often tend to focus on what went wrong. Do your best to let your partner know what you need rather than focusing on what went wrong. The more specific the better. Let them know exactly what you need without being demanding and making orders. Instead of threatening, try something like, *"I need you to help out with this because..."*

Being kind is so often overlooked. You got into this relationship because you love one another, make sure you reciprocate that. When we get into arguments we can quickly forget about all the things we love about our partners, this makes it easy to put each other down. It really goes back to the golden rule, treat others how you would like to be treated, the same goes for your spouse. How would you like to be treated if you made the same mistake? Although you should not have to ignore every problem that arises you should be able to voice your concerns without fear of emotional outbursts from your partner.

Our bodies are wired with millions of years of evolutionary instincts. Our minds can not tell the difference between a real threat and a perceived threat, therefore we often act the same to a perceived threat as we would a real, physical threat. It is a natural response to get into fight mode when your sympathetic nervous system is triggered by a threat, whether real or perceived. When you are in this state of mind, you should not be trying to resolve a conflict. When your body takes over and your mind is not thinking logically about the situation, you are also portraying to your partner through your body language your anger and frustration and it will likely only escalate the situation and make things worse.

There are four main areas of emotional ability and several strategies within those areas that you can work on to better improve your communication while emotions are high. Many of the strategies you can use for keeping your emotions in check are similar to those we talked about in the previous section on how to communicate through conflict. At some point or another in your life and in your marriage, you are going to experience emotions and feelings[23] that are difficult to get across to the other person.

Your perceived emotion is the ability to accurately read your own emotions. When you are aware of your emotions you can determine whether the emotions stem from something internal or external. When you have a low ability for perceived emotions, you will tend to take external factors and turn them inward. Perhaps your car didn't start this morning and that will then ruin your entire day even if other good things happen. You might also get into a bad mood more easily if others around you are in a bad mood. Just the opposite is true, however. If you have the high emotional ability you will be able to maintain a good mood even if there are external factors that are going on that are not so

---

[23] https://everydayfeminism.com/2014/02/effectively-communicating-feelings/

good.

When looking at strategies to help us in this area of emotional ability, you should work through your feelings independently. When you can determine what kind of feeling you are having and name what a feeling is (we will get to that in a minute) you should be able to figure out why you are feeling that way. You are not looking to blame your feelings on anything or anyone, rather find a source of why you are experiencing those feelings. When you realize the source of your feelings, such as a specific situation or event, you will be able to more easily communicate that feeling to others.

But before you bring up your feelings to another person, you need to be able to work through it on your own. Have you ever needed to speak with someone about a serious matter but when it came down to actually having the conversation you had no idea where to start? You don't need to create some crazy outline of talking points, but having a general idea of the things you need to talk about and how to approach them is a much better way of starting a serious conversation.

It can be very helpful to talk with friends about how you are feeling about something before bringing it up to your spouse. But you must be intentional about who you go to talk about your issues. You don't want to talk with someone who will give you unsolicited advice or run back to your partner about your conversation, rather someone who understands effective communication and will ask you questions to help you clarify your feelings. If you do not have friends who are effective communicators, you might want to try meditating or journaling about your feelings to get better clarification for yourself.

When you are facilitating your emotions you are getting ready to make decisions. You need to be able to assess your emotions and find a useful way to put them together. Facilitating includes identifying, or naming your feelings/emotion or thought, getting to the root cause of it, and then deciding how to act upon it. Being able to do this will help you keep cool when emotions are high in just about any situation. It will also help you better understand your partner and come to a common ground.

There are a few strategies helpful in this area of emotional ability that will help you facilitate your emotions and thoughts in order to move on to understanding and managing your emotions.

Understand that you are worthy of your emotions. Have you ever apologized for feeling a certain way? *"I'm sorry I'm feeling a little blue today honey, I'll try to be in a better mood tomorrow."* Know this: you are allowed to have feelings and you don't need to apologize for them! Many people when they get emotional feel the need to apologize for the feelings they are experiencing and become apologetic. This leads to feeling as though our feelings do not have merit or worth, which can become a large barrier in being able to express yourself comfortably.

You shouldn't invalidate your feelings, you can't help the feelings that arise. Although someone can act on a bad feeling, your feelings themselves are never bad or wrong. You shouldn't apologize for having feelings.

Acknowledge and name your feelings and thoughts. When things get emotional our thoughts and feelings can become clouded and lumped together. Try to acknowledge what is a thought and what is a feeling and give them labels. Think of it like you are inputting data into a computer. Label each emotion you are having as a feeling or a thought. You THOUGHT he didn't care about you, which made you FEEL angry. When you label them and turn them into data, it can be much easier to let them move on.

Now that you have already established that you are worthy of having feelings and should not have to apologize for them, it is time to acknowledge the fact that you are having them and name them or put them into some type of category. We can often tell if the feelings we are having are bad or good, but what does "bad" or "good," actually mean? Try and drill down into what your feeling actually is. Are you feeling good because you are satisfied with your work performance for the day? Are you feeling bad because you are feeling inadequate because of how your spouse has been acting toward you lately?

This is a great time to break out the dictionary or a thesaurus and figure out what you are actually feeling. This is where a journal might come in very handy. Take a few minutes each day to write about how you are feeling, the root cause of that feeling, and other words to describe that feeling other than good or bad.

Here are a few words that might be helpful that signal anger:

- Provoked
- Shameful
- Unstable
- Agony
- Damaging
- Harsh

Here are a few words that might be helpful that signal being happy:

- Gleeful
- Delighted
- Thankful
- Gratified
- Energetic
- Spunky

As you can see, there are many ways to describe how you are feeling other than the general good or bad.

Now that you are aware that you shouldn't have to apologize for your emotions all of the time. you should also know that your feelings do matter to others. While we can get so wrapped up in our feelings in our own minds, it is easy to forget that other people care about our feelings and emotions. We might often feel that our feelings do not matter to others based on how they react or respond to us. Or we might not realize that others care about our emotions because we have not yet figured out how to work through them on our own.

When people care about their well-being, they also care about their feelings in return. When people don't care about your well-being, they are often toxic relationships and don't deserve your time anyways. You should be able to identify a toxic relationship when you realize you are putting in way more effort into the relationship than the other person. This can happen in both friendships and relationships. Someone who validates your feelings and loves you should always be willing to listen to your feelings, without judgment or pushing their agenda on you.

When you can understand your emotions, name them, validate them, and know that they matter, you can help to predict how you will feel in future situations. While there are many situations you encounter day to day, many of them are much in the same. Dealing with an upset boss because something was not finished on time, dealing with an upset child because they didn't get what they wanted, dealing with an upset spouse because they had a bad day. While these are all different situations, they can be handled in much of the same fashion.

Be solutions oriented. When you can understand your emotions and where they are coming from, you can come up with a plan on how to handle them in future situations by using a solutions-based approach. Instead of becoming stuck on your emotions and dissecting them, come up with a plan on how to handle them. If you are discussing your feelings with your significant other, address your feelings with "I" statements (more on that in just a second), then focus on how the issues can be changed in the future. Address how you are both feeling, acknowledge and name the feelings, then find a way to move forward and address the issue so it does not keep arising.

"I feel unheard when you forget to take out the garbage. What are your thoughts on that? How can we work to change that in the future?"

These emotional abilities that we are discussing don't necessarily go in a linear order. While it is wise to be able to understand where your emotions are coming from before you jump into a conversation on them, you might also need to manage them first before doing anything. There are many ways to manage your emotions and feelings through self-regulatory actions such as, controlling your breathing, repeating a mantra, concentrating on your body, creating some space between you and the person you are talking to, and using "I" statements or expressing your point of view.

Control your breathing. As simple as it sounds, breathing can help to calm yourself down immensely. Using simple mindfulness techniques can help to create major changes in tense situations. Learning to breath is such a straightforward technique and can be used in any situation. If you notice that you are becoming tense, really try and focus on your breathing. Be mindful of how you are feeling as you breathe in and the air fills your lungs and how you feel when you exhale. This will help to divert the physical signs of distress and help to keep you centered. Experts suggest that you count your breath when you inhale and exhale.

Repeat a mantra. This works well for so many reasons and is another very simple technique to implement. Come up with a saying that you find helpful and reassuring to say to yourself when you are feeling emotionally charged. This can be anything that you feel will work for you. *"This too shall pass,"* is a very popular mantra for when times get rough.

Concentrate on your body. When you are getting emotional and worked up about things, sitting still can make it worse. While you might alarm your partner if you suddenly get up in the middle of a heated argument and start moving around, it might help to diffuse the situation. You also don't need to make very large movements in order to help provide some relief, you could try something small like touching your thumb to your fingers or shaking your leg. Getting up and moving your body activates the thinking part of your brain. If you do feel the need or want, to stand up and walk around for a bit, simply tell your partner how you are feeling. *"I feel like I need to stretch my legs, mind if I get up for a bit?"*

Create some space. Your emotions tend to be very tense when you are initially feeling them. The more time you give yourself to process them and work through them on your own, the less intense they will be and the better you will be able to effectively communicate your emotions. So if things are feeling a little heated and you need to step away, let your partner know that. Tell them that you need to walk away for a bit use the bathroom or get a drink of water, or even just let them know that you need to process what is happening before you can continue the conversation.

Use "I" statements. I touched on this just briefly when we discussed being solutions-oriented and understanding your emotions. Using "I" statements focuses on expressing your point of view of the situation and takes the blame off of the other person. They are direct, honest, and promote self-accountability when used correctly. Instead of focusing on what the other person may or may not have done, focus on how you feel when that person does something. Doing this will help you to own your feelings and experience rather than centering the conversation on someone else's actions.

"I feel [this way] when you [do this] or when [this situation] happens."

Approaching a conversation in this way helps to

be more neutral and not seem like you are accusing the other person of something, thus avoiding them getting defensive. While also helping you to become more in touch with your feelings and emotions and what is affecting them.

This technique can also work on yourself when you are trying to figure out where your emotions are coming from. Instead of focusing on something negative about yourself or your (perceived) inadequacies, address your feelings with "I" statement when you are trying to acknowledge and name your emotions.

"I feel [this] when I [do this]."

We all have feelings and we all experience emotion in some form or another.

Sometimes to the best of our efforts, we just need

to let our partner vent and get something off their chest. In this case, your best bet is to sit and listen to what they have to say and let them say what they need to say. Remember, it is whether you respond or react, that will lead to escalation or de-escalation of the situation.

Chapter Summary

Learning to become a better communicator all starts with being a better listener. Using reflective listening is a great way to get started on your path to understanding better. Simply repeat back what you heard the person say in your own words.

"Ok, so what you are saying is..."

You should easily be able to tell if you have understood what their message was. There are many tools that you can use to effectively communicate with your spouse.

- Choose the **timing** of your communication carefully. Don't try and have a serious conversation with someone when they are hungry, angry, lonely, or tired.
- **Respond** to your spouse and the argument

rather than reacting to it, this will give you the power to end the argument. Take a neutral stance and don't get defensive or place blame.
- **Focus** on the conversation at hand and do your best to cut out all the noise.
- Do your best to **clarify** exactly what you mean from the beginning of the conversation.
- Ask more **questions** in order to understand your partner. Don't interrogate, remain neutral and seek to understand.
- Use **technology** to communicate appropriately and stay away from it when trying to have a serious conversation.
- Create **habits** with each other.
- Intentionally find **wonder** in your relationship.
- Regularly engage in **positive physical touch.**
- Eliminate miscommunication by **mirroring**

back what your spouse is saying to you. *"So what I hear you saying is...is this correct?"*
- If a conversation seems to be getting out of control, **S.T.O.P.** This means stop the conversation, take time out, own your own part, and offering a peace offering.

Communicating through conflict and emotion can be very difficult. There are certain steps that you can take to help work through these difficult times:

- Don't use criticism as a way to get your message across, this will only cause more harm than good.
- Use empathetic statements to let your spouse know that you understand how they are feeling.
- Remain calm and think about your partner's good qualities.
- Use "I" statement to express your feelings: *"I

feel hurt and like I am not being heard when you forget to take the garbage out."
- Focus on the current matter at hand rather than bringing up the past.
- Focus on telling your partner what you need rather than what went wrong.
- Just be kind to one another!

Our bodies cannot tell the difference between a real and a perceived threat, therefore, we respond the same using a flight, fight, or freeze response. It takes time and practice to learn how to control your emotions when trying to effectively communicate, but there are some additional things you can add to your toolbox to help:

- Work through your feelings independently before talking to your partner about them.
- Facilitate your emotions by identifying them, naming the feeling/emotion, getting to the

root cause of it, and deciding how to act upon it.

Learning to facilitate your emotions is another skill to add to your toolbox. There are several strategies to help you in facilitating your emotional ability:

- Don't apologize for your feelings or emotions, don't invalidate them, you are worthy of them.
- Acknowledge the feelings you are having and name them.
- Write about your feelings regularly, how you are feeling, the root cause, and descriptive words (such as "shameful" rather than "bad").
- Understand that your feelings also matter to others.
- Use a solutions-based approach to help manage future emotions.

→ **Here is an example**: *"I feel unheard when you forget to take out the garbage. What are your thoughts on that? How can we work to change that in the future?"*

There are also some physical things you can do to help manage your emotions and physiological responses when trying to communicate through conflict and or tense situations:

- Control your breathing.
- Repeat a mantra.
- Concentrate on your body movements.
- Give yourself some space.
- Use "I" statements.

In the next chapter, we will focus on the keys to a healthy and lifelong marriage, cultivating, rebuilding, and repairing trust.

Chapter Three:
The Key To a Healthy And Lifelong Marriage: Trust

Trust is a delicate thing, it can take years to earn and seconds to break. In this chapter, we will cover some heavy topics that many couples struggle with. Trust can be easily broken through many acts, such as lying about finances or infidelity. You will learn how to cultivate lasting trust in your marriage, what you need to build a safe environment, how to repair and rebuild your relationship after trust has been broken, how to save a marriage when dealing with trust issues, and how to survive after infidelity has taken place.

Cultivating trust can happen when you are initially building trust with one another or after something has happened where the trust needs to be repaired. You don't enter into marriage with one another expecting to get a divorce or be cheated on. You marry each other because you love one another, want to grow old together, and want to trust, love, and respect one another. All too often we hear about all the negative things revolving around marriage. Gossip with your girlfriends and chats with his guy friends might make us feel vulnerable about the level of trust in our relationship. In order to build trust with your significant other, there are some core things that you can work on.

Always be transparent...even when it makes you feel uncomfortable. You need to talk to each other about things that might not be easy. For example, if one of you handles the finances and they are not great at it, you need to communicate that to the other party. Remember, you took a vow to be together through thick and thin, so you need to have those uncomfortable conversations with one another and not try to hide things. When you hide things that will only lead to a breakdown in trust between you and your partner.[24] Smaller things can lead to bigger things, then before you know it, an affair. I know that might sound a little extreme, but it happens.

---

[24] https://ourpeacefulfamily.com/trust-in-marriage-how-to-build-rebuild-restore-spouse-wife-husband/

When after so many years of hiding simple things from one another feels normal, then taking a big leap like that isn't such a big leap. Even if the conversation is uncomfortable, even if you think the other person is going to become made about it, transparency is key to building a trusting relationship.

Talk about your common goals. As a couple, you each have your own individual goals and goals you want to reach together. Perhaps one of you wants to finish college, or you both want to pay off your debts or buy a new house. As you make, meet, and change your goals your vision and focus will change over time. Try to connect on a regular basis to talk about your goals and the vision you have for each other and your family. What are the steps that each of you are taking to reach those goals? What are you both doing to make that vision a reality? Talking about goals with each other, especially long-term goals, will help to solidify trust in one another that you are both in this for the long run.

Give each other your own space. We all need a little time for ourselves, and no, being at work or running to the grocery store alone doesn't count. Being able to give each other space is crucial in developing a trusting relationship. Just think about if your spouse never let you go out of the house alone, that doesn't feel very trusting, does it? Although you might really love spending time with one another, also encourage each other to enjoy individual hobbies or getting together with friends or family. You might even need this once and to de-stress from each other if there has been tension or arguments. Spending some time apart from one another helps to build trust while also giving time to recharge and be the best person we can be when we come back.

Share in your common values. If you are already

married, I am going to assume that you at least share some common values. Values can mean anything from how to handle your finances, your faith, and especially your children. Not sharing common values when parenting together can be extremely taxing on a relationship. You should be able to talk to one another about the values you are passionate about so you can focus your energy into those priorities together. If you have had a disagreement, knowing that you are on the same page with your values will help you become centered again as a couple and know that you can trust in one another and have each other's backs.

Put your story together on display. Marriage is a journey, one that you should be proud of. Sometimes when you are in the thick of daily life, in an argument, or losing trust in one another, a visual reminder can help you remember why you are in this relationship in the first place. Display pictures and mementos of the big and the little events. The big events like your marriage or the birth of your children. As well as the little things like your favorite coffee at work because he knew you were having a bad day. This helps you to remember the trust you have built with one another and how you should continue to work on it together, every day.

Promote and build a safe environment in your marriage. Having a safe environment can mean many things. We generally seek safety when there is a perceived or real threat to our physical or emotional well-being. In order to effectively communicate with one another, both parties need to feel physically and emotionally safe.[25] Even though there might not be screaming or physical violence, you might still feel a threat of that as your brain can not tell the difference. If there is any kind of actual physical or emotional

---

[25] https://www.focusonthefamily.com/marriage/strengthening-your-marriage/how-to-create-an-emotionally-safe-marriage-environment

abuse, get to a safe environment as soon as possible.

When someone feels that their emotional safety is being jeopardized, they will react. This reaction could be leaving the room or lashing out at the other person. The goal is to be able to create an environment of effective communication and intimacy rather than one you want to escape from filled with animosity. You can help to foster intimacy in a relationship, even after an argument, by creating a space that feels safe for both of you.[26] When you are both relaxed and in a peaceful state, sharing and openness will happen. When you are both feeling safe, you shouldn't have to force intimacy or work overtime to create a connection. It takes an emotional strain on both of you when you are trying to stay closed and shut off from one another than it does to open up to each other.

---

[26] https://www.focusonthefamily.com/marriage/communication-and-conflict/the-power-of-healthy-conflict/creating-a-safe-marriage

When you feel hurt, you disconnect. When your spouse is able to admit and apologize for their wrongdoings you often don't want to disconnect any longer. You want to open your hearts and connect with them again. After an argument has ended your main goal should be to reconnect with one another in a safe and loving environment. When we feel emotionally safe we are able to open up who we really are, all the while knowing that our significant other will still love us unconditionally.

You must also realize that you each have a personal journey that you have brought with you into your marriage. Perhaps from previous romantic relationships or from your family and or friends. If in a previous relationship you were always put down or belittled, it might be difficult for you to accept any criticism without feeling like you are being attacked thus initiating your flight or fight response. Try to understand why someone reacts the way they do. Is it the way you are approaching them? Trauma from a previous relationship? Or do they simply not have the emotional availability to discuss what you want to discuss at that point?

We each have the power to control our behaviors, thoughts, feelings, and beliefs. You can change the way you are showing up in a relationship and effectively express to your spouse how you feel about a situation. Be respectful of their feelings and their past experiences in order to build a stable future.

While we have each been on our own individual journeys when you get married you also take a journey together. However, in order to really be on a journey with your spouse (not just taking a different journey alongside them), they must give you permission and their cooperation. Have you ever met a married couple that seemed more like roommates than an actual couple? This is not taking a journey together, this is taking separate journeys at the same time. You can not grow together and have effective communication if your spouse shows no cooperation.

We talked about respecting each other's boundaries in making love and respect work together. But we didn't discuss boundaries in regards to emotional safety. Setting boundaries can mean a lot of different things. Perhaps when you are getting into a heated argument there needs to be a boundary set of something physically being between the two of you, like a counter. Or perhaps if one of you is feeling emotionally unsafe, they have to be allowed to walk away without being called out for it or followed. It is going to take some time to figure things out. Don't try and establish your boundaries when you are in the middle of a heated discussion but rather when you have both had time to think and discuss with one another what will work best for you as individuals.

Now that we have established how to cultivate trust in a relationship, what do you do when trust has been broken? There are many reasons for trust to be broken in a relationship. Broken promises, lies, infidelity are all things that can quickly erode trust in a relationship. Just because trust has been broken does not mean that it is indefinitely over. While it can certainly be difficult to repair trust in a marriage once it has been broken, it is not impossible. If both partners are committed to working on repairing trust, it can be done.

Repairing broken trust is not easy, it takes a lot of time and effort on both parties. Many couples get stuck here because they do not know to pick up the pieces and move on. It doesn't matter if you are the one who broke the trust or not, repairing and rebuilding trust is a two-way street that you must both journey on together.[27]

Now the process of working to repair trust that I am going to outline below can help when trust is broken in just about any situation. Perhaps your spouse (or you) had an emotional or physical affair or lied about finances. While these things may not be all-encompassing of ways that

---

[27] https://www.verywellmind.com/rebuild-trust-in-your-marriage-2300999

couples break trust, many things can fall under those categories.

The first step is always the most difficult. Before you can both start to repair your relationship, the offender needs to own up to their mistakes and the other party needs to know all of the details. Whomever the offender needs to own up to whatever mistakes they made and not try and make excuses or try and justify their actions. When you try and justify or make excuses for your actions it will only make things worse by upsetting the other spouse more.

When something happens and we don't know all of the details we either stay naive about things or assume the worst case scenario. If one spouse has made a mistake, they should be open and honest about the situation and be able to answer all of the other spouse's questions, no matter how uncomfortable. This will help to lay everything out there and will not allow the other spouse to make assumptions about the situation.

You might think it would be a good idea to minimize the damage done if you leave out some of the details about the trust breaking event. While that is a logical thought process, there is a major downfall. Say you leave out a detail (or several), you are working on repairing and rebuilding your marriage, things are going great, then BAM! Those details somehow become revealed. Now you have broken trust again but this time around it is only going to be more difficult to repair and rebuild if you are able to at all.[28]

Forgiveness does not mean forgetting. In order to work towards repairing your marriage after a break in trust, you need to forgive yourself and forgive the other person. This is a very important

---

[28] https://www.fatherly.com/love-money/rebuild-trust-marriage-major-screwup/

part of the process to regain trust and emotional well-being for you both. When something happens, we try and find explanations in order to help understand the situation. The non-offending partner might blame themselves, or the offending person might try and blame the non-offending person. Perhaps we feel there is something wrong with us and that is why this happened and if there was some way to fix it, it wouldn't happen again in the future. Many people have difficulties forgiving someone if a break in trust has occurred. If they forgive them they might feel that they are getting off easy or that they are showing weakness by forgiving their actions.

Forgiving yourself, whether or not you are the offender, shows that you still value yourself and know that you are worthy of love and respect. Whatever the situation, how the other person behaved has nothing to do with you but is rather a reflection of them. Forgiving someone isn't about them, it is about your emotional well-being and freedom. If you can understand the other person's perspective, it might be easier for you to take any focus off of yourself and begin to heal. Forgiving someone and making peace with the situation is easier when you look at the whole person rather than view them as their mistakes and or flaws. There are still many good things about them and the reasons that you love them. Try and focus on those aspects by seeking and looking to forgive someone's past mistakes.

When someone hurts you, it makes you angry, and that is totally understandable. It is ok to be angry at first. Even the smallest bit of trust that is broken can lead to major issues, including mental, emotional, and physical health issues. While for some it might be their coping mechanism to stuff anger down inside and not talk about it. Or perhaps it is expressed in other outward actions such as a decreased appetite, trouble sleeping, or greater levels of irritability. If you are the non-offending party, you need to reflect inward and focus on the feelings that you are having. How is your life being disrupted? What questions or doubts do you have about the incident?

As the offender, what kind of emotions and feelings are you having? You should be able to openly express them in a safe environment without judgment and scrutiny. In order to heal, you need to be able to effectively communicate with one another.

It's easy to question commitment when a betrayal of some kind has happened. Perhaps you are wondering if your marriage is worth saving or if you are still right for one another. It is very simple to say that you are going to do or change something, it is something else entirely to actually follow through with it. If you begin to make empty and unfulfilled promises your spouse is not going to trust you and you are not helping to repair the relationship.

You can help show commitment and keep your promises by promoting empathy within the relationship, sharing in each other's pain and frustration, showing remorse (if you are the offender), and allowing space for each other to be able to validate and acknowledge your emotions and hurt feelings. You should be able to let each other know what you need from one another in order to heal and move forward in your relationship.

Focus on using "I" statement and avoid using blame focused words like, "always," "never," and so on. The trust breaking situation occurred because you didn't have effective communication in the first place. Now is the time to change that and build a stronger relationship.

Building a strong relationship doesn't happen overnight. You know the old saying "Rome wasn't built in a day," that holds true for so many things. This is especially true when trust in a relationship has been broken. While it is no fun living with someone who is ticked off at you for what you did, just saying sorry might not be enough to get things back on track. When trust has been broken, it can take a very long time to repair what has been broken. This goes right along with showing commitment and letting your spouse know that no matter how long it takes to get things back, you are there for them. Trying to force someone to forgive you on your timeline is not going to work. They need to be able to work through their emotions and feelings in their own time.

Your relationship might be different and you

have to be ok with that. While that might be a distressing thought, you have to realize that even after the relationship has been repaired and rebuilt, it might never quite be the same as it was before. Even if there is forgiveness, it might not be total forgiveness. It is also not something they are likely to forget any time soon either. If that is how things play out, you have to be able to accept that and move forward the best you are able to.

When you are working to rebuild trust in a relationship, you need to make sure that your words and your actions are one and the same.[29] It's like trying to lose weight, you can't say you're not going to eat cake while shoveling into your mouth. That just doesn't add up. When your relationship is shaky, you need to grasp onto that stability wherever and whenever you can. You can show your spouse that you are serious about

---

[29] https://www.psychologytoday.com/us/blog/living-forward/201609/how-rebuild-trust-someone-who-hurt-you

changing when you do what you are actually saying and do it on a consistent basis. This also shows them that you want to earn that trust back and you are willing to work for it.

Now that you fully realize just how much time rebuilding your trust with one another is going to take, you need to be able to set realistic timeframes and goals for your rebuilding process. You both need to make a conscious decision to forgive or to be forgiven. While it may take some time, letting go of the past and committing to moving forward is going to be key in healing. Of course, each party has to want it to work between you. You can't have one spouse doing all of the work while the other sits back and expects things to change without them having to do anything.

There is also a lot of growth that takes place when moving through rebuilding trust in your marriage. Often when a betrayal of some kind happens, it is because of some underlying issues that need to be resolved. In order for those issues to be resolved, they need to be identified and worked through with both spouses, not just the offender. You both need to explore your thoughts and feelings about the matter and not stew over them. This will only cause the trust to remain broken and resentment to build.

When rebuilding trust in a marriage, you must both learn to trust one another while also trusting in yourselves. You have to have trust in yourself in order to trust in others. People often fear to trust in others again once they have been hurt because they do not want to be hurt again and become humiliated or ashamed. It can also really takes a toll on their self-esteem when they are always fearful of their partner breaking their trust again. They also might feel that they will be seen as being weak if they stay with someone who has broken their trust. It generally takes a lot more strength to stay in a relationship (obviously not an abusive one) and to work through things rather than leave.

While you, as the non-offending partner, might do everything possible work on trusting someone again, there is no certainty that they will not break your trust again. The same could be said for the other hand. Even if you were the offender and you do everything in your power to try and gain someone's trust back, there is a chance that they will never fully trust you again. When you give someone to trust, there is always a bit of faith and chance involved. You have to have faith in them that they will not break your trust again, but you also have to take the chance that they might.

Once you both have fully committed to working on your relationship together and rebuilding trust with one another, you get to start over. Treat your relationship as though it is new. You must tell each other exactly what you want and need and don't expect to read each other's minds. In order for your relationship to move forward in a healthy way, you need to make sure you are not withholding trust from one another. Even though you might still be feeling fear or anger with your spouse, in order to emotionally reconnect you have to openly give trust again. You need to work together to build a healthy marriage and set common goals for your relationship. Perhaps it is time to implement a regular date night, work on a five (or 25 years) plan together. Check in with each other on a regular basis to see how you each feel your relationship is progressing.

One of the fundamental things that you need to understand about trust is that it is a secondary issue, not the primary problem in most relationships. A lack of trust happens as a result of something happening. When someone has hurt us, by cheating or lying about something, we develop a lack of trust for that person because we are afraid that the same (or similar) thing is going to happen again. You then start to question yourself and your spouse and lose trust in them.

Although your issues are unique to you as a couple, couples everywhere have dealt with the same kinds of issues. You are not a snowflake in this case. Whatever issues you are facing as a couple has already been had and solved by many other couples. I am saying this to give you hope. While your issues are unique to you, the situation and core issues themselves are not unique. Here are nine principles that will help you to save a marriage with trust issues:

Be positive and how your spouse gratitude. Your mindset needs to be in a position to implement all of the other principles. Many couples feel that their situations are very bad in addition to being extraordinary. A painful relationship is not that same as a bad relationship. In order to be positive, you need to put your relationship, as it is right now, as being good without changing anything. In comparison to others' relationships, yours is in the middle. There are always going to be couples that are worse off than you and couples that are better off than you. It is simply a shift in your mindset. Look at the things in your life and relationship that is good. What is it you are grateful for?

Don't forget about your guiding values! Take a good look at your relationship. Why are you in it in the first place? Most likely you both share core values that initially brought you together. Remind each other of what those guiding values are and how they affect your relationship.

This is where your humility comes into play. Your willingness to change it on you. While you might feel the need to point out the things that your spouse needs to change, that can cause further friction. Notice and make a note of the things that you need to change and work towards fixing your own issues and guide your behaviors.

You need to be able to forgive your spouse. This involves your willingness to let the other person change. Don't focus on holding history over their head or continue to hold a certain image of them in your mind. If someone truly wants to change, they have the power to do so.

Whether or not you are the offender, what kind of respect are you going to practice? We might feel the need to be respected, but giving respect is just as important. Even though it might be difficult to respect your spouse in certain situations, you should always be a respectful person. Giving respect is not about them, it is about you.

Choose loving behaviors and actions. Now, this does not refer to mushy, romantic love. Love is a choice, it is about how you show up for one another. There really is no neutral ground, there is either love or hate to some degree. You have to make the choice to love one another. You need to take responsibility for your own choices and commit to your choice, and you should be choosing love if you want to rebuild trust and repair your relationship when trust has been broken.

Compassion here has to do with kindness. When you are compassionate about something, you have a willingness to suffer for it. What are you willing to commit to this relationship? When you are able to move past all the blaming and finger pointing, how important is your relationship to you? Are you willing to suffer and step outside of your comfort zone in order to make it work?

Rebuilding and repairing a marriage after trust has been broken is a lot of hard work. Elevating your relationship requires effort on both parties. Everything that is worthwhile is going to require effort and is going to be a bit of an uphill battle.

Now I know that might be the last thing on your mind when you are trying to repair broken trust, but it is so important! Good old fashioned, wholesome recreational activities. Try to establish a date activity at least once per week if at all possible. Don't just endure your life together, have some fun! When you are having fun together don't focus on the problems that you are trying to resolve, focus on the moment and just be with each other at that moment.

Many people often describe infidelity as a deal

breaker for a marriage. But what if it were possible to survive and even thrive in your marriage after infidelity has happened? This, unfortunately, is something that many couples have had to deal with. It is difficult and uncomfortable to talk about and can be even more difficult to heal from. It is possible to come out on the other end with a stronger, healthier, and more satisfying relationship if they make a commitment to work through things, apply the principles we are going to talk about in this section, and make a conscious choice to work it out.

While infidelity, in and of itself is unhealthy and destructive to a relationship, it does not have to be the end of your relationship. You can use this experience to strengthen your relationship and communication skills and increase your love for one another. Here are four principles to focus on in order to move past the infidelity and start to rebuild and repair your relationship with one another.

First and foremost, end the infidelity. Yes, I know this seems obvious, but it is a critical step in moving forward. You can't move forward and heal if you or your spouse are still in having an affair. This can be a very difficult step for the offender as there have been many dynamics that have to lead up to the other relationship developing.

Completely sever the connection. This goes hand and hand with the first step. While some people might end an affair, they may still continue to speak with that person. You have to make sure that everything that gives an opportunity to be in connection with the person that the infidelity occurred with, has to go! Remove the contact from the phone, block their number, unfriend and unfollow them on all social media. It doesn't matter if you feel like you are being rude, be rude! You are doing this to save your marriage not worry about saving face with someone you had an affair with. Don't stress about what other people are thinking about you, you can't control their thoughts, you just need to worry about you and your spouse.

Create complete transparency in your marriage. Infidelity is built on secrets and hiding things from one another. If you have accounts on social media, either delete them or give your spouse access to everything, including your phone contacts and text messages. Give them access to all of your email accounts, any bank accounts that they might not have known about, anything and everything. Yes, this might feel like an invasion of privacy and very intrusive, and it should. Marriage is an intimate experience, therefore you shouldn't have a problem being up in each other's business unless you are trying to hide something! You should be sharing intimate and sacred things with one another and be ok with it. Complete and total transparency.

Make the time to communicate with each other. In order to repair a marriage that has gone through infidelity, there as to be a lot of talking and a lot of communication. Communication goes beyond simple conversations. Make time to talk with one another and be able to do so while feeling safe to discuss things that make you feel vulnerable. Couples might find that it is helpful to go to counseling or hire a coach to help facilitate this process. You don't want to just be fighting every time you are trying to talk, learn and practice communication skills.

Once trust has been broken in a relationship it can be very difficult to get back. When one spouse breaks trust, it can be one of the most damaging things they could do to the relationship. As humans, we are all broken in some way and we use those broken parts of us to hurt those that we love. One of the best ways to rebuild trust is through consistent integrity and doing what you say you are going to do. Having integrity has to do with what you say and what you do perfectly matching up, again and again. Having integrity is like making deposits into your trust bank account. When you have taken out a large withdraw from breaking trust, you have to build it back up again with deposits of integrity.

Whenever we are hurt or offended, we create a story in our minds and create an attachment to that story, often times this can be a story of a victim. When you tell yourself that you are a victim, you are giving the person who hurt you all the credit in your story. What you should be doing is giving yourself the credit and telling yourself a hero story. Are you a hero for forgiving them and moving on to a better relationship with them, or are you a hero for letting them go and getting the toxic person out of your life.

When you are hurt in a relationship, you have two choices, to let that relationship go or to fix it and move forward. If you choose to let that relationship go, then you have to be able to release that toxic relationship without grieving about it. If you are going to choose to fix the relationship and move forward together, you have to make sure you are both going to make an effort to repair and rebuild the relationship. Either way, you should be able to forgive that person and move forward, whether by yourself or with them.

Chapter Summary

Trusting in your spouse is so important to a healthy and lifelong marriage. However, it is very delicate and can easily be broken. There are things you can do to cultivate trust in your marriage and repair and rebuild when it has been broken.

- Always be transparent, even when it makes you feel uncomfortable.
- Talk about your common goals.
- Give each other your own space.
- Share your common values.
- Put your story together on display.

In order for a relationship to thrive each partner must also feel that they are in a safe environment. These safe environments can feel jeopardize with a real or perceived threat. We also bring baggage into a relationship which can influence our behaviors. You are also on a journey together, but you need to give each other permission to take part in each other's journeys and cooperation with one another. You must also be able to establish boundaries with one another in order to create a safe environment.

What happens when trust has been broken? How do you fix it?

- Realize that repairing trust is a two-way street and takes a commitment from both parties.
- Own your mistakes. Don't make excuses or try to justify your actions.
- Spill ALL the details, don't hold anything back.
- Forgive one another.
- Release your anger.
- Be committed to keeping your promises.
- Realize that it is going to take time to repair

your relationship when trust has been broken.
- Your relationship might never be the same and you have to be ok with that.
- Work for consistency in your words and actions.
- Set realistic timeframes and goals for rebuilding trust in your relationship.
- Tell each other exactly what you want from your relationship.

It is possible to save a marriage with trust issues. Your marriage is not too far gone, here are nine things you can work on to revive a marriage that has suffered a break in trust:

- Be positive and show gratitude!
- Don't forget about your guiding values.
- You have to be willing to change.
- Forgive your spouse for their wrongdoings.
- Practice respect whether or not you feel they

deserve it.
- Choose loving behaviors and actions.
- Show compassion to one another.
- It is going to require a lot of effort, work for it.
- Don't forget to have fun with each other.

When infidelity has happened in a marriage, there are four big things that you can do to make sure your marriage is going to survive it.

- End the infidelity.
- Completely sever the connection.
- Create complete transparency in your marriage.
- Make the time to communicate with one another.

Just like we all bring baggage into our relationships, all of the broken pieces we bring into a relationship we use to hurt one another with. When you are hurt in a relationship you have one of two choices to make. You can either let that toxic person go or you can do your best to try and fix things.

In the next chapter, you will learn all about how to keep a marriage alive and stay in love with each other.

Chapter Four: Keeping Your Marriage A.L.I.V.E. and Staying in Love

It doesn't matter if you have been married for a year or for 50 years. It doesn't matter if you have kids, young kids, together, they are grown and moved out, or never had kids at all. Marriages can become stagnant. Things can become mundane and boring. Perhaps you feel more like roommates rather than lovers. A stale marriage does not have to be a death sentence. All it takes is some communication skills and a little effort to keep the love alive in your marriage.

Let's use ALIVE as an acronym for how to keep your marriage thriving.

A is for attitude! Your attitude is not how you feel about things! Your attitude can certainly affect how you feel, but your feelings are not your attitude and your attitude are not how you feel. Your feelings are the result of something that has happened. Your attitude is your stance on how to handle what has happened. If you are aiming to keep your marriage alive, you need to assume a positive position about your marriage, even if you feel that things are not going great. The way things are in your marriage right now, just think of this: yes, things can always be better, but they could also be worse. The position that you take on your marriage depends on which way you are looking in relation to how it could be. If you are looking at a marriage that is much worse, of course, yours is going to look much better. If you want to keep your marriage alive and well, assume the attitude that it already is.

L stands for love. Not sappy and romantic love, while that is wonderful in and of itself, I am referring to the choice of loving your spouse. There are two sides to the coin in a relationship, love, and hate, good and bad. While it works on sort of a sliding scale, ultimately there are two sides. You have to make the conscious choice to love your spouse. There really is no neutral options, you either do things out of love or out of hate. Now hate doesn't really mean hate in the way that you would think, it could also mean resentment, nasty, unpleasant, loathsome, disgust, animosity, apathy, hostility, antagonism, pain, revenge, grievance, spite, disdain, the list goes on. On the other end of the spectrum, love can mean many things and manifest themselves in many ways. It could mean tenderness, emotion, appreciation, affection, fondness, friendship, lust, passion, respect, attachment, fidelity, enjoyment, and so on. You have to make a conscious effort to love one another and act out of love rather than hate.

I is for inspiration. We each bring in energy to our relationship, it is either positive or negative, much like the love or hate we chose to act on. With inspiration, you are also making a choice as to whether to destroy or to build your relationship. What things are you doing to destroy or build your relationship? There are many factors that go into this. Your thoughts, your energy, your touch, and your language, all help to either destroy or build up your relationship. Inspire and lift not only your relationship but your partner. Don't tear each other down and criticize one another.

V, in our acronym, stands for virtue. There will come a time (or many times) in your marriage where you might have to choose between what is easy and what is right. When that time comes, make sure you choose what is right and be virtuous. The principle is simple, do what's right. The act of virtue can be very difficult. Do what is right, even when and especially when it is hard!

The final letter in our ALIVE acronym is **E**, which stands for energy. We all have a certain energy and vibration to us. When we are being positive and constructive, we "vibrate" higher than when we are being negative. We want to seek out people that vibrate that same as we do. This makes us more compatible with that person. When one person is vibrating with good, positive energy and the other person has negative energy, there is not as much compatibility. If you are feeling that you have very negative energy (are angry about something or upset) try and bring yourself up to a higher frequency by doing things that are filled with positive energy. For example, listening to music that is filled with love and positive energy rather than angry or depressing music. This can easily be applied to your relationship. When you are operating at a higher level, it will almost force your spouse to come up to your level. While it might feel uncomfortable to do this at first, they should, in time, be able to either come up to your level or meet you somewhere where you both will have better energy.

In the rest of this chapter we are going to go over

the psychology on staying in love every day, how to handle verbal abuse from your husband, how to get your spouse to pay attention to you (even if the football game is on), and what to do if your partner is driving you crazy.

We have already established that when we talk about love, we are not talking about passion or lust, we are talking about the choice of love. Our love goes through different levels of maturity. These levels of maturity can be defined by looking at chemistry, clarity, and commitment. Chemistry refers to feelings like passion and lust. Clarity looks at how your values, personality, and intimacy will work with one another. And of course, a commitment really looks at the ability to work through difficult times and situations and be able to come out on the other side of it with a marriage that is strong and intact.

The first level of maturity in a relationship is

yearning. Yearning love is those fairy tale endings, the "falling in love" part of a relationship. It is high in chemistry, often with lots of passion and lust. Where you just can't keep your hands off of one another.

The next phase in a relationship is all about earning love. Earning love takes place, after the honeymoon, so to speak when real life sets in. This is the stage where the clarity of the relationship is much higher and becoming more defined. This is where goals and expectations within the relationship are getting worked out. The commitment, at this point, might be questioned. Is this relationship really built to last? Are you able to work through your stuff and come out on the other end? Sometimes, after the yearning stage, the relationship might end. They think that they have fallen out of love with one another, when in reality that has actually just moved into another stage of their relationship development.

The enduring stage of a relationship is the final stage. While the term "enduring" might sound negative, it actually is not. This is where you will find people that have been married for a very long time. There is no question that they love one another and that they are committed to one another. Chemistry at this stage in the relationship might be irrelevant. We all go through physical changes as we age and our relationship ages and there might not be as much lust, and that is ok. The clarity at this point is crystal clear. You know exactly what the purpose of this relationship is and are well versed in each other's values and personality. The commitment, as I'm sure you can guess, is stable and lasting.

In order to keep a relationship going, you need to be able to feed your relationship in several areas. The chemistry you feel with one another, the clarity you have on the purpose of your relationship, and the commitment you have towards your partner and your relationship need to be fed all the right things in order for you to keep a relationship alive and stay in love with one another. If you starve your relationship of vital nutrients, so to speak, it is going to wither away into nothing. Think of it like a glass of water that you have to keep pouring into. If you only fill it up halfway and stop pouring in, it is never going to reach its full potential.

You need to be able to feel safe with one another, to be vulnerable, and to express how you feel without fear of rejection or retaliation. You need to trust in each other, to build and feed the trust in that relationship. You need to show appreciation for one another. Showing gratitude and appreciation for one another is so important. How can you feed the sense of appreciation and gratitude in your relationship? You need to show respect and respect one another, simply, be kind and treat your partner as you would want to be treated. Acknowledge how your partner contributes to the relationship and validate that your life is better because they are in it. You need to encourage one another and be able to give each other courage and confidence. You chose the relationship that you are in on purpose, you should be able to demonstrate that you are dedicated and committed to your partner.

If you are experiencing verbal abuse in a relationship, there is hope to fix it. The verbal abuse topic can go both ways. Women can experience verbal abuse from their husbands and men can experience verbal abuse from their wives. It's unfortunate that abuse happens at all, but the reality is that it does. No one deserves to be abused, whether emotionally, physically, or verbally. PERIOD! You should not tolerate abuse of any kind. You deserve kindness, respect, and dignity and is a completely reasonable expectation.

In this section, we are going to talk specifically about how to handle verbal abuse from your husband. Often, verbal abuse can lead to physical abuse. Just because verbal abuse is taking place, this does not mean that your husband is a bad person, they just lack the skills to properly communicate their feelings. If this is the case, you can be the bigger person and teach them how to properly communicate with you. Domestic abuse is a very big problem and it causes a ripple effect into other areas of life and in our communities.

Due to the high correlation of verbal abuse and physical abuse and domestic violence, if any of these are occurring, safety should be the very first concern. Don't be afraid to stand up for yourself and speak up if you are in a verbal abuse situation. If you are in a situation where you are experiencing physical abuse and domestic violence, you should seek outside help immediately and get away from the situation and the offender. Different communities offer different resources. But regardless of where you live, you deserve respect and deserve to be safe.

When it comes to verbal abuse, the person offending takes shots at the "victim." This means that they are hitting you where they know it is going to hurt and they are doing it on purpose. Perhaps they know you are sensitive about your weight, they will intentionally make snide and hurtful remarks about your weight to bring down your self-esteem. There are three steps that you can use to handle these situations when someone it taking shots at you; identity, verify, and accept.

Identify the abuse. Here is where you can use your stellar communication skills to identify what is going on. There are times when people are verbally abusive and they don't even realize it. Perhaps they were brought up in a home where verbal abuse was the norm for them and they don't know any different. They simply might not be aware that what they are saying is considered abusive, abrasive, or that it is bothering you.

When this happens, use your "I" statements!

"I feel _ when [this] happens."

You are going to take the focus off of them and put it on yourself. If you go at them stating that they are doing something wrong, they will likely get defensive and shut down or lash out. This is not going to help the situation at all and could possibly make it worse.

While the premise of the identifying step might be simple, it is probably not going to be easy. It is likely that this person has been either intentionally or inadvertently using verbal abuse for a long time and it will be difficult for them to admit it as well as difficult for you to talk to them about it.

Verifying the verbal abuse holds a lot of power. You need to verify that if what they said/did was what they were intending on doing. Simply ask them if that is what they intended. For example, *"I feel_when you say [this], is that what you intended?"*

Most of the time when this happens, the person you are talking to is going to back peddle. Either they are going to try and cover their butt if that is what they actually meant or they will genuinely express that is not what they meant. They might also try and turn it back on you saying that you are too sensitive or that what they said was somehow your fault.

However, it doesn't really matter what their response is. Either way, you move onto the next step of acceptance.

Accept their response, no matter what it is. While you are going to accept their response, you are not going to accept to be continually verbally abused. There needs to be an end to that! All you need to do to accept the response is say, *"ok."* That's it. While your tone will probably vary depending on the situation and what the response was, your response should just be an *"ok."* Don't react to the verbal abuse, most of the time if it is intentional, that is what the offender wants you to do, they are trying to get under your skin. Don't let them! This can be a very powerful psychological tool. This sends the message to the other person that they do not get to treat you with disrespect and if they do you are going to call them out on it. Even if you don't directly say that to them, that is what you are communicating to them.

While many times this can happen with husbands towards their wives, this strategy can be applied in many situations. Wives being verbally abusive towards their husbands. Teens and adult children being disrespectful towards their parents. Or a boss being verbally abusive to their employees. If you are experiencing verbal abuse, give these three steps a try and see how it can change the dynamic of the relationship.

Now that you know how to stop verbal abuse, how do you get your spouse to pay attention to you? Generally speaking, men are more distant than women and women need to feel that they are being paid attention to more. Now, this is a very board gender generalization that can not be applied to every couple. In some relationships, the wife is more distant and the husband needs to feel that they are being paid attention to. Or perhaps both partners feel that the other is not paying enough attention to them and they need to find ways to connect with them so they feel that they are getting their needs for attention met. In any situation, there are some very simple and easy things that you can do to get your partner to pay more attention to you.

Even if you think they might be too busy, there are some very simple strategies that you can implement in order to get your spouse to pay more attention to you. It comes down to sending messages. For five days you are going to send them five different messages each day. This can be talking to them face to face, over an email, via text message, or a note in their lunchbox. Get creative if you want to. The five messages you are going to send on a daily basis are appreciation, connection, elevation, love, and acknowledgment.

You need to let your spouse know that you appreciate them and the things they do for you and your family. A simple *"thank you"* for doing something around the house is a great way to show appreciation. Now, if your marriage is really on the rocks, you might be thinking that there isn't anything you appreciate about your partner right now. But stop and think about it for a minute. Do they go to work and help pay the bills? Do they pick up the kids from school or take them to their extracurricular activities? While they might not be going out of their way to do something spectacular, like secretly getting an oil change for you while you are at work, there is likely at least something they are doing that you can show them an appreciation for.

The message doesn't have to be grand or over the top. A simple and genuine *"thank you for going to work today so we can afford to live in our home,"* will mean a lot to someone, especially if they work a job they don't particularly enjoy. If you have problems saying things in person, write them a little note and leave it where they are sure to see it. Try and be as specific as you can when you are giving your message of appreciation. Don't just say, *"oh I appreciate you,"* let them know why. Even if you think they already know that you appreciate them, tell them!

Don't focus on this that your partner is not doing. This is only going to make them feel criticized and make the situation worse. When you criticize or nag someone this is going to cause them to pull back from the situation and you are going to push them away. When you show someone they will appreciate it and will start to pay a little more attention to you.

When you got into this relationship, you both shared some type of connection. This could have been a hobby, political views, movies you both love, many different things. However, over time those connections can fizzle out. Now is the time to revive those and to reiterate those connections. Communicate with your partner something you have in common, something you have similar views on, something you are on the same page about.

For example, if you hear your spouse talking

about something that you know that they have strong feelings about, and you agree with them about it, let them know that you agree with them. While you are not directly saying *"this is my connection message to you,"* you are still sending that message of connection to them when you are agreeing with them about something. Or perhaps you found out something new about them that they like that you also like, let them know that.

Elevation refers to lifting the mood. It is really such a bummer when someone is being negative all the time. It can often bring down other people's moods when someone they care about is being negative and is in a bad mood all the time. If your spouse suffers from being a downer, try and elevate their mood by being elevated yourself. Just as negativity can be contagious, so can positivity. Smile, use delightful humor, point out funny or humorous things to your partner.

You can even share humorous videos you find on social media with them.

Earlier we talked about love as being an act rather than a feeling and it is on a spectrum with hate. You have to make the choice every day to show up and act in a loving way. There is no neutral, there is no indifference, there is either acting in love or acting in hate. Love is also compassion, empathy, respect, and caring for each other.

The message of love can be a direct one, where you are specifically saying *"I love you,"* to your partner, or it can be indirect. An indirect message is often an intentional and loving interaction with each other.

Acknowledgment can often get confused and mixed up with appreciation. While in many situations you can kill two birds with one stone, so to speak, by acknowledging and showing appreciation to your partner in one message. In general, husbands what to feel valued and important. Their wives need to let them know that they are doing a good job. The acknowledgment message that you should be sending your partner is that your life is better because they are in it.

These are the five messages you should be sending your partner for five days. Do this and it is likely that you will start to pay a lot more attention to you in a much more positive manner.

If you are a man, I'm sure you have either said this or have heard your male friends say this (that are in a relationship), *"my woman is driving me crazy!"*

If you are a woman, the same holds true. You

have either said this about your man or your girlfriends have said it about their man. Just as we learned earlier in the book, men and women might say the same thing but it means two completely different things.

Generally speaking, when a man says *"my woman is driving me crazy,"* that translated into *"I just can't seem to please her/do anything right!" "She keeps telling me to do this and this..."* There are numerous things that could mean, but ultimately a man says that when he seemingly can not meet his partner's expectations.

When a woman says, *"my man is driving me crazy,"* that generally translates to something like, *"he isn't listening to anything I say," "he doesn't do anything that I ask of him,"* and so on.

When your spouse is driving you crazy, there are several steps you can take to help yourself work through it.

When you are feeling upset and like your partner is driving you crazy, breathe. Take some time to slowly inhale through your mouth and exhale through your nose. Try and count on the inhale and count on the exhale. Your exhale count should be about twice as long as your inhale. I know breathing might sound so simple, but it is a skill. If you are not used to it, you might feel light headed at first, don't worry, this just means that you are getting more oxygen to your brain than it is used to.

Breathing helps to calm both your mind and your body. When you breathe you are getting more oxygen to your body and you are focused on your breathing so your mind is not on a million other things. When you get worked up, your body goes into flight or fight mode. Your physiological responses kick in and your brain and body think there is a threat, even when in reality there is not. But remember, your brain and your body can't tell the difference between a real threat and a perceived threat.

Science has shown that when your flight or fight response is triggered, there is less blood flow to the prefrontal cortex, which is the part of your brain responsible for decision making, problem-solving, and rational thought. When you breathe, you are stopping the flight or fight response and getting more blood flow to the brain and are able to solve problems and think logically.

When your partner is driving you crazy, it is not your job to understand their actions right away, but to love them. If you initially understood them, then they wouldn't be driving you crazy now would they? You each see things differently, you should at least be able to understand that and not try and focus on knowing that you are right (if that is indeed the case), move on, and choose to love one another.

There are many different things that you can do in order to move towards understanding each other. The great thing is, once you can understand one another, you will both feel less annoyed and irritated with each other. What your spouse is doing might not make sense to you, but it makes sense to them, in their world. First, you must seek to understand your partner, then seek to be understood. When you are seeking to understand your spouse, you should be listening to them. Actually, listen to them, don't just sit there like you are listening and while they are taking trying to come up with your rebuttal to whatever it is they are saying. You don't need to agree with them, you just need to try and understand what they are saying. You can easily do this by repeating what they said back to them in your own words.

Chapter Summary

It doesn't matter how long you have been married, at some point your marriage is going to feel stagnant. Here are five key factors to keeping your marriage ALIVE!

- A is for attitude. Your attitude is the stance you take on what happened and how you handle it.
- L is for love. Make the choice to love your spouse.
- I is for inspiration. Inspire and lift up your partner with your thoughts, energy, touch, and language.
- V is for virtue. When it comes to choosing what is easy and what is right, choose what is right.
- E is for energy. Vibrate with positive energy rather than negative energy.

Within every romantic relationship, we all go through different levels of maturity which are classified by chemistry, clarity, and commitment. Chemistry refers to passion and lust, clarity focuses on intimacy, values, and personality, while commitment is the ability to work through difficult times.

- Maturity level #1: yearning-this is high in chemistry and low in clarity and commitment.
- Maturity level #2: earning-this is lower in chemistry, higher in clarity, but commitment might be questionable.
- Maturity level #3: enduring-chemistry is irrelevant, clarity is well defined, and commitment is stable and lasting.

When verbal abuse happens in a relationship, there are three things that you can do to handle it.

- Identify the abuse using "I" statements.
- Verify if the verbal abuse was intentional.
- Accept their response, no matter what it is.

Even if you think they might be too busy, there are some simple strategies that you can implement to get your spouse to pay attention to you. For five days send five messages of appreciation, connection, elevation, love, and acknowledgment.

Just as with trying to communicate through conflict and emotion, there are several things you can do when your spouse is driving you crazy.

- Breathe.
- Love first, understand second.

In the next chapter, we will cover how to successfully destroy your marriage and how to bring it back from the brink of divorce.

Chapter Five:
10 Ways to Successfully Destroy a Marriage (and How to Bring it Back from the Brink of Divorce)

There are many ways in which to destroy a marriage, but it ultimately comes down to a lack of communication. You don't see couples who have great communication skills getting divorced now do you? Of course not! They are able to work through whatever issues they might be having and repair, rebuild and make their relationships stronger. Having said that, let's count down the ten things that can destroy a marriage (that all tie back to poor communication).

An insensitivity to requests and preferences of your spouse.

This can be from big to little things. From leaving the toilet seat up to smoking. These preferences and requests are important to your spouse for one reason or another, you should pay attention to them.

Sucking all the fun out of everything.

If you haven't experienced this with your spouse, I'm sure you have experienced it with someone in your life. It doesn't matter the situation, but that person just sucks the fun out of every situation and is always too serious about things. You might even be the fun sucker in the relationship. You focus too much on the things that you should do or must do that you forget about having fun. Lighten up a bit and have some fun with life!

Plain old laziness

We can all be lazy once in a while. Maybe it has been a really only week and you just want to chill out for a bit but your spouse thinks you are being lazy. Or perhaps your spouse is just not willing to step up and do their part in the marriage, around the house, or with the kids. This can quickly kill a relationship when you feel like you are the only person actually doing anything. This also goes for a lack of appreciation. Laziness can sometimes be coupled with a disconnect of a realization of how much work the other person is actually putting in on a daily basis.

Being mean.

Being mean can be a big relationship destroyer. I'm sure you've heard the old saying, you catch more flies with honey than vinegar. This is so true in a relationship. You aren't going to make friends when you are mean, and you aren't going to get across to your spouse when you are being mean.

Choosing hateful actions.

We have gone over this concept multiple times now in the book. Love is a choice, hate is a choice. While you might initially think that love and hate are feelings, in reality, they are choices. You can choose to act in love or act in hate. Choosing hate can destroy a marriage quicker than just about anything. There are three steps to choosing hate that can ruin a marriage:

- Assuming the worst about that person. You might not know what their intentions are, but in order to choose hate, you have to really focus on what is going wrong.
- Practice pride. You know you're right no matter what. Hold your position and really dig in your heels, don't yield!
- Coming up with ways to retaliate. This is where things can get interesting. Come up with ways to hurt your partner, to punish, and to destroy them.

This is where you grab your emotional shovel and dig up the past. You use every opportunity you can to throw something they did back in their face and use these things to diminish the relationship. Just as with choosing hate, there are four steps to forming and holding a grievance:

- You get hurt. There is some level of implied hurt in all relationships.
- You over-personalize the offense.
- You blame someone or something else for how you feel.
- You create and retell a victim story about how you got hurt. This might even include spreading around social media and revel in your hurtful situation.

Always having to be right.

This is not thinking that you are right, but knowing you are right! This often leads to treating one another terribly. This tends to put you in a tricky relationship in relation to your spouse. It has been shown that approximately 70% of issues in relationships are unresolvable. This does not hold true just for couples that are already in trouble but also for couples who have great relationships. When you think that your spouse it the problem, that right there, is the problem. It's how you think about the situation, your stance on the problem that is the problem. If you are taking a negative stance and always thinking that you are right and your spouse is wrong, that is what is causing the problem.

Using thoughts, behaviors, and language that is profane.

While profanity generally refers to swearing, in this situation is also means taking something that should be sacred and making it profane. This covers both thoughts and behaviors. This can be anything from addiction, criminal behavior, swearing (at your spouse), infidelity, and so on. Profanity refers to all things that can diminish the relationship. This can also include a detachment from morals and values and in reality, should be the foundation of the marriage.

Always taking a position of negativity.

This means, by choice, taking a position of negativity. Thinking that marriage is bad creates the outcome of bad marriage. It doesn't really matter how bad or good you think your marriage is, it can always be better. You are more likely to improve your marriage when you don't NEED the improvement. I know that might sound a little confusing. Your spouse is more likely to work with you when you feel and portray that marriage is good rather than bad. So if you want to destroy your marriage, take a position of negativity. If you want your marriage to improve, even if you already think it is good, take a position of positivity.

One thing that you have to realize is that the pain is not "out there," it is inside you. When you realize that the pain you are experiencing in your marriage can be controlled by you, that changes the way you view the marriage and its landscape. This is not how most people view a "bad" marriage, they view the pain as being internal, within the marriage rather than within themselves. This might then make them feel that they should leave because the pain is within the marriage. The pain is internal if you leave it will only follow you to your subsequent relationships.

We are programmed with certain views and values of marriage. If you had parents that stayed married and miserable or your parents divorced, you are more likely to do what they have done in their relationship. While many of us might not remember the first ten years of our lives very vividly, our subconscious remembers everything. The way your parents were together in the first ten years of your life has literally programmed how you will be in your marriage. If there was emotional abuse, kindness and compassion, all of those things you experienced from your parents and how they interacted in their marriage in the first ten years of your life carry over into your adult life.

When you get into that flight or fight mode and your prefrontal lobe shuts down, you are more likely going to do the same type of things that your parents did in their marriage. Until you are conscious and aware of the things that are happening and the things that have happened in your past, you are not going to be able to control how you react to certain situations. If you are a man and your father had a temper and blew up in the face on the conflict, you are highly likely to do the same. If your parents raised you with many values and taught you compassion, you are likely to respond to situations very differently than someone's parents who did not.

When you are able to realize what you are doing subconsciously, you can then work towards changing those behaviors. When spouses learn to communicate with one another, magic can truly happen in their relationship. They realize that they are not their parents and they can take decisions to act or react in a certain way.

But is it really possible to save a marriage on the brink of divorce?

Every marriage has problems and issues. Couples that are miserable and couples that are highly satisfied with their marriages have the same percentage of unresolved issues. The problem is not that all marriages have problems, the problem (or solution in some cases) is how they handle the problems.

There for four things that couples do that put them on the miserable side of a marriage rather than a happy and satisfied side; criticism, defensiveness, contempt, stonewalling. The couples that are doing this in their relationships are handling issues in a negative manner and will only continue to be miserable. It's a very simple concept, but in order to change the dynamic, you should do more of what works and less of what doesn't.

Many times we have this assumption that things would be better if your spouse just changed and did what you have been asking of them. How about you try and do a little experiment to see if after five days you can start to create some positive changes in your marriage. First off, assume 95 percent of the responsibility of your marriage. Try and do this for a solid five days rather than you do your half, I'll do my half, fifty-fifty type scenario. Considering you are going to be assuming 95 percent of the responsibilities, that means that your spouse should only be doing about five percent. So most likely, they are already doing enough!

This is probably playing out a little bit differently in your mind. You might be thinking that there is a whole load of things that your spouse could be doing better, but that does not serve your relationship, that mindset and thought that the process is not helpful! As soon as you start to identify what your spouse could be doing better, they are going to take that as criticism. Instead of focusing on all the things that your spouse could be doing better, why not focus on the things that you could be doing better? This will dramatically change the dynamic of the relationship and you will find that there are plenty of things that you could be working on rather than pointing out the things your spouse could be working on. This is a great way to bring a marriage back from the brink of divorce.

Do you recall earlier when we talked about how to get your spouse to pay attention to you? This is a great time to refer back to that. If you recall, for five days you send your spouse five messages that include appreciation, love, connection, elevation, and acknowledgment. If you have already tried that experiment and found it helpful, try another one that focuses on gratitude. For five days write down 25 things that you are grateful for. But wait, there is a catch. Half of your 25 things have to be about your spouse and you can't repeat any of them. Yes, this exercise might get a little difficult, but in the end, you will have 125 things on your list that you are grateful for, roughly 63 of which are about your spouse. Now if your marriage is on the rocks, this exercise is not going to be easy, but it will be extremely helpful. But focus on how your marriage is right now, not how you want it to be or how it was.

When your marriage is on the brink of divorce it can be difficult to put in the extra effort to try and make things better. But if you truly want to make things work, you have to do things differently. Give your spouse "gifts" of appreciation, connection, enlightenment, and elevation through your words and actions. Send them the message that you value your relationship and are willing to work for it. Go out of your way to serve them and your relationship. Saying you are going to work for them isn't enough. If you were divorced, you would probably still go to work, so that really isn't for them. So think about various ways that you can serve your spouse that will communicate to them that you are grateful for them and you value your relationship together.

We talked about this earlier, love and hate are not really felt, they are actions. Considering they are actions, this means that we always have a choice to love or hate someone when we interact with them. If you are not making actions towards the love side, you are choosing actions towards the hate side. Now when someone makes the choice to hate you, you choose to love. Yes, this sounds weird and difficult, but hear me out. Hate happens in a relationship when there is an offense between two people. Just think about how wars get started, someone offended someone else and they responded in a hateful way. Hate fuels hate and love fuels love. When someone makes a choice to do something towards you, what kind of decision are you going to make? Are you going to let their hateful decisions fuel hateful decisions from you or are you going to choose love?

Now when someone says or thinks that they hate their spouse, it is really not that. There are other underlying factors that make them think that they hate their spouse or that their spouse hates them. "Hate" in a relationship generally comes from typical human weakness or a position of feeling threatened. Think about it. If you hate your spouse because they cheated on you, that has to do with their weakness and your feeling threatened and scared. Just because someone is acting in a hateful way does not make them a bad or evil person. So keep these things in mind when someone says they hate you or you tell someone you hate them.

If you are experiencing hate from your spouse, go back to the gratitude exercise that I previously talked about. For five days write down 25 things that you are grateful for, with half of them being about your spouse or your marriage without repeating any! Then at the end of those five days, show them your list. Intentional gratitude changes your mind and your focus. This is your chance to influence your spouse when they are being hateful. While you are doing this gratitude exercise, also make sure you are sending your spouse some messages. They can be obvious or subtle messages, but they should be messages that you value the relationship, that your life is better because they are in it, and send them the message of specific appreciation.

It can be really amazing when you start changing your attitude when someone is being hateful towards you how they can quickly change their tone. Perhaps they don't even realize that they are acting in a hateful way towards you. Or perhaps they have hurt you in some way and are looking for your forgiveness. At some point, they are going to need to say sorry for hurting you, but they might not know how or where to start.

It is not really a matter of if your spouse or partner hurts you, it is a matter of when. We are all human and we all make mistakes. We are all broken in one way or another and we bring those broken pieces into our relationships and use those broken pieces to hurt the ones we love. But how can we say sorry when that happens?

When you need to apologize to someone for hurting them you need to be sincere in your apology. Don't just apologize out of the obligation to, do it because you want to and because you mean it. You also need to be specific for what you are apologizing for. Just sincerely saying you're sorry isn't enough. Your partner should know exactly what you are apologizing for even if you think they already know. When you apologize in a sincere manner and you are specific and have come to terms with what you have done, the focus shouldn't be on you. Yes, I know that sounds counterintuitive. Focusing on the person that has been hurt helps them to validate their feelings and let them know that you realize that your actions negatively affected them.

Avoid trying to *"but"* your way out of things. When you apologize for your actions, there should be no *"but"* in the sentence. This will only lead to you trying to justify your actions and make excuses. Using *"but"* takes the focus off the person you hurt and could, essentially, place the blame on them. With every mistake that we make, we should use that as an opportunity to learn from our mistakes. If it is appropriate, share what you have learned from this mistake with your spouse and what your commitment is in the future. Doing all of this when you have made a mistake will help to build your relationship and move forward in a positive and healthy way. But what should you do if lies and infidelity have happened in your marriage?

Principles determine all of life's outcomes. What does this actually mean? No matter how bad or messed up you think your relationship it, there is nothing that can't be resolved with the correct application of the proper relationship principles. Even if you think you have the worst relationship out there, you have the ability to create a change, even if you are the only one in the relationship making an effort. There are nine core principles that you can apply to any relationship to help save it even from the worst lies and infidelity.

Take a positive stance. Your mindset is incredibly powerful and it can determine many of the outcomes in your marriage and any relationship you have in your life. Take a stance of positivity even if your relationship is in the gutter. Even if your spouse is a negative nelly, think of your relationship, as it currently is, in a positive light.

Reconnect with your values. At some point in your relationship, you shared values, otherwise, you would never have gotten together. Why are you with each other, or why did you first get together? What is the purpose of your relationship? This all taps into the values that you share. Sometimes life gets in the way and we have forgotten about why we started this relationship in the first place. Try and renew your values to each other or focus on the values that you once shared.

Have humility. It doesn't matter if you think that you are right, you need to have the willingness and the openness to change. So many times arguments happen because spouses are not willing to budge and they KNOW that they are right! Instead of focusing on who is right, you should focus on what is right.

Again, we are all human and we all make mistakes, some bigger or smaller than others. Forgiveness is the gift that we can give ourselves and our spouse so that we may move on with the relationship and create something better with one another. Stop digging up things from the past and holding it over each other, it doesn't do you any good!

Respect has nothing to do with your partner and everything to do with you. Respect is about your integrity, your personality, and your character. Even if you are not receiving the respect you should still give it.

Make the choice of love not hate.

To be compassionate you are empathetic and can put yourself in your spouse's shoes. It is about kindness and caring for another person.

Elevation requires effort. In order to raise your relationship up, it takes effort. If you don't put in the work the relationship will go down. You can't stop pouring in when the glass is half full and expect it to fill up on its own. The more damaged the relationship the more work it is going to take to elevate it up to the point you want it to be at.

While repairing and rebuilding a relationship after lies and infidelity is a lot of work, you should also be able to have fun with each other. What's the point in putting in all this work if you can't have a little fun along the way?

These principles are very powerful in creating massive positive change in a relationship. But be aware, don't try and teach them to others who you think might need them, even your spouse. Just as when you criticize your spouse, trying to give them unsolicited relationship advice is only going to backfire. Do your 95 percent and do your part in creating change in the relationship. Your spouse will change when they are ready and then you will be there to provide them with these resources and be able to effectively communicate with them.

Chapter Summary

There are many things that people can do to destroy a marriage but the main issue is a lack of effective communication. Here are the top ten things that you can do to destroy your marriage:

- Have an insensitivity to requests and preferences from your spouse.
- Sucking the fun out of everything.
- Laziness.
- Being mean.
- Choosing hate.
  - Assuming the worst about that person.
  - Practicing pride.
  - Coming up with ways to retaliate.
- Acting with disrespect.
- Form and hold grievances.
- Always having to be right.
- Using thoughts, behaviors, and language that is profane.

- Always taking a position of negativity.

One thing you must realize when it comes to pain in your marriage is that it is internal. The pain you are experiencing is not "out there," it is in you. You are programmed to act and react in certain based on how you were raised and how your parents handled conflict in their marriage.

70% of all issues in a marriage are unresolvable. This holds true for both blissful and miserable couples. There are four things, however, that keep couples miserable:

1. Criticism
2. Defensiveness
3. Contempt
4. Stonewalling

There is a trick to changing the dynamic of a relationship, do more of what works and less of what doesn't. Here is a little experiment that you can do over five days to try and create some positive change in your relationship:

- Assume 95% of the responsibility of your marriage.
- Write down 25 things that you are grateful for, half of them have to be about your spouse/marriage, and you can't repeat any.

If your spouse expresses that they hate you, that really isn't accurate. Generally, when someone expresses hate it comes from a position of feeling weak or threatened.

At some point in your marriage, one of you is going to hurt the other. When you apologize for it, leave the "but" out of it. Be sincere in your apology and use these nine core principles to save your relationship from even the worst lies and infidelity:

1. Take a positive stance.
2. Reconnect with your values.
3. Have humility and a willingness and openness to change.
4. Give the gift of forgiveness.
5. Show respect even if you think the other person doesn't deserve it.
6. Make a choice of love, not hate.
7. Be compassionate.
8. Be willing to put in the work.
9. Have fun and enjoy each other's company.

Here is one final tip when it comes to creating massive positive change in your relationship: don't try and force your spouse to change. When they are ready they will make changes on their own or ask for your help.

In the next chapter, I will cover the nine-step action plan for positive communication in marriage.

Chapter Six:
ACTION PLAN For Positive Communication In Marriage

Wouldn't it be great if someone could just hand you a step by step outline on how to make your marriage work better? Well, you are in luck, here I have outlined nine key steps that focus on how to make your marriage work.

We talked about these nine principles briefly in the previous chapter but I wanted to go much more in-depth with them here and give you some actual real-life strategies to make these principles work for you in your marriage. Now the great thing about these principles is that they will work 100% of the time in every situation. I know, that sounds like a tall order considering marriage problems vary so drastically. But it is true! If you work and apply these principles to your marriage, it will work!

No, it doesn't matter if you think you have a great marriage (although I can bet if you thought that you wouldn't be reading this book…) or if you think your marriage is on the outs. It's a shocking statistic but roughly 70% of all problems that arise in a marriage are unresolvable. Now you might think to yourself, "well why the heck even try then?!" Problems in this sense refer to conflicts. This happens because when you bring two different people together conflict is bound to occur at some point due to their differences. This does not make their differences bad, it is a lot of times what brings couples together. In order for the relationship to develop in the first place, we have to have differences.

Now, these unresolved issues are present in both miserable couples and happy couples. There are four telltale signs as to if a miserable couple is still headed towards divorce or if they are able to turn things around in their marriage. If there is a lot of criticism (perceived or intended), defensiveness, contempt, and stonewalling. If couples are habitually using these tactics to try and resolve their issues and are not willing to change these behaviors, they will likely end in separation and divorce.

Obviously, those tactics don't work in a

relationship and only cause more damage. Here is a fascinating idea, what if you did less of what doesn't work and more of what does work? There is no problem that can't be resolved with the proper application of these nine principles.

1. *Being Positive*

Yes, I understand that being positive can be very difficult when you feel like your marriage is crumbling. Being positive is about how you choose to see your life and the energy you bring to it. Think about this for a minute, while there are many couples that have a much better relationship than what you currently have, there are also many couples that have a much worse relationship than what you have. While it might be easy to compare your situation to others, don't!

Being positive is also about being grateful.

Quick Tip: Start a gratitude journal. Think about the positive qualities of your relationship and your spouse and record them in your gratitude journal. If you are just getting started, write down one thing each day about your spouse or your marriage that you are grateful for, in the present moment. Don't try and bring things up about how good things used to be or how great they might be in the future, be grateful for the present. For example: *"I am grateful for my husband because he cooked dinner tonight while I took our daughter to dance."* Be specific about what you are grateful for!

2. *Shared Values*

At some point you shared values, things that are important to you, that is why you got into this relationship in the first place. A lot of times when an individual in a relationship is looking to channel their values they will turn to their faith, meditation, or prayer to center on the purpose and the values.

Quick Tip: Add this in your journal. What are your values? What are the values that you shared when you got together? Then brainstorm some ways that you can work on those values together.

3. Having Humility

When you have humility you are not prideful, you have a modest view of your self-importance. When you lack humility and you hold onto your pride you tend to treat others badly because your pride comes first. So now is the time to give up your need to be right all the time and start connecting with your spouse. You also have to be willing to change your behaviors that are causing disruption to the relationship.

4. Forgiveness

There is a lot that goes into forgiveness. You have to be willing to allow other people to change and give up your demand for a better past. Think about it. You can't change the past, you can't change what you or your spouse did or didn't do, you can only work on the present to improve the future.

Continually bringing up things that have happened in the past is only going to continue to cause harm to your relationship. Forgiveness is also a two-way street. You have to be able to forgive your spouse for whatever it was that they did and you have to also forgive yourself for things. This could be a mistake that you made or it could be for being a "victim." Many times when a spouse does something we can blame ourselves for our faults somehow causing them to make this mistake. So you must forgive yourself too. You are allowed to have your feelings but you must not dwell on them and beat yourself up over them.

5. Giving Respect

You should give respect to everyone, even if you think they don't deserve it. Respect is not about the other person, it is about you. Showing someone respect even when they do not deserve it says a lot more about your character than theirs. So even when it is difficult, even when you think they don't deserve it, and even when they think they don't deserve your respect, give it! Be a respectful person no matter what.

6. Choosing Love

I've talked a lot about this in the book, the choice of love or hate. Think of love and hate as being on a line, love on one side, hate on the other. Now in the middle, there is no neutral, just a tipping point between the two. With every action, with every word, you are making a choice to either love or hate. Cheating on your spouse is a terrible choice. Even though you might feel like you love them, your actions were hateful.

Giving your spouse a kiss before bed, that is a loving choice. Choosing love is crucial to a successful marriage. When you make hate choices over love ones you will quickly be headed for disaster.

7. *Compassion*

Compassion is another choice. Compassion is being kind and caring. While it might be a love choice to make your spouse dinner, it is a compassionate choice to get them their favorite wine to go with dinner because you know that they have had a rough day. Do you see how practicing compassion can really make a huge positive impact on a marriage?

8. *Put in the Work*

You can read this book and make two choices, either go, *"oh, that was a good book with some useful information,"* and then never actually USE the information. Or, you could take the principles outlined in this book and apply them to your marriage. Fixing a marriage takes work. Whether you have a little or a lot of work to do, marriage is not a destination, it is a journey. You can't stop in the middle of your journey just because it gets a little difficult, you have to keep going and put in the work to make things better and continually improve.

9. *Good Old Fashioned 'Fun'*

You should be having fun in your life and in your marriage. Find things that you both enjoy doing together, have a date night, go hiking, visit somewhere new, just have fun together. What's the point in spending your life with someone if you aren't having fun?

Now I know this might sound like a lot of work to do, and trust me it is. It is not likely that your marriage fell apart overnight, it isn't going to get fixed overnight either. It can be very overwhelming for someone who has been in a frustrating marriage for a long period of time to suddenly flip and switch and change their behaviors. Focus on one or two things at a time and work up to them. But here is the real trick…don't force your spouse to do these. When you come at someone and tell them they need to be doing something, you are likely to be met with withdrawal and skepticism. While you can certainly give them a copy of this book and let them know that you are working to change things, you can also just go about your life and make the changes and see what happens. It is very likely that your spouse is going to notice a change and start to reciprocate your behaviors.

Chapter Summary

I am going to make a bold statement; use the nine principles listed below in your marriage and they will work 100% of the time and in every situation to create positive communication.

- Be positive!
- Focus on your shared values.
- Have humility.
- Give forgiveness.
- Show respect.
- Make love choices.
- Be compassionate.
- Put in the work!
- Have fun together.

Don't try and force change in your relationship. Do your best to make the changes you can and your spouse should follow suit.

Final Words

I'm sure it comes as no surprise how much work a marriage takes. There is a rather large learning curve when living with, and learning to communicate with another person. When there is a breakdown in communication this can often lead to a breakdown in the relationship which unfortunately often results in divorce. It's inevitable that couples will argue as 70% of all issues in a marriage are unresolvable. However, with a fully stocked communication toolbox, arguments can be resolved quickly and your marriage can thrive.

You understand at this point that men and women communicate differently and there is nothing wrong with that. The problem comes from a lack of understanding of what each is saying. Men and women might say the exact same thing but it will mean something completely different.

Some of the key points that we covered in the book that I hope you practice and add to your communication toolbox are:

❖ Realizing the differences between male and female communication styles. Men are logical and 'to the point', whereas women can often solve their own issues just by talking aloud about them.

Learning to effectively communicate with your spouse can be a game changer in your marriage. One of the simplest things to do to get started is to repeat back to your spouse what you heard them say in your own words. While your spouse says this:

"You never take the garbage out, I always have to remind you!"

You can respond to this:

"What I am hearing you say is that you are upset because I forgot to take the garbage out again and you get frustrated when you have to continually remind me. Is that correct?"

You can even take it a step further and ask your spouse what you need to do to fix the problem and how to avoid making it a recurring issue.

"What kind of solution can we come up with so you , I won't forget and you won't continually have to remind me to take out the garbage?"

Quick tip: setting reminders on your phone or smart home device can really help with this one!

- ❖ With every message, there is a sender and a receiver. The sender sends message A, but it must first be encoded, pass through physical or mental noise, then be decoded by the receiver. This can often result in message A being received as message B.

❖ You can encourage positive communication by listening, seeking to understand, staying focused on your audience, maintaining appropriate eye contact, and smiling, being positive, and saying yes!

❖ Learning to hone your body language can increase your likability. Learning to understand the body language of others can help to break down barriers and help to figure out what someone is really trying to say.

❖ Love and respect are two emotions we can not get enough of. Love is for those close to you while you should respect everyone, even if you think they don't deserve it.

- ❖ In order to become a better communicator, you need to learn to first become a better listener. An effective listener hears what the person is saying, understands the body language and tone of voice, and properly decodes the message.

- ❖ When you are trying to communicate to your partner how you feel, use "I" statements to shift away from a blaming mode.

While the concepts and principles in this book are simple, the work you have to put in to implement them are not. In order to communicate effectively with your spouse and improve your marriage, you have to build up your communication toolbox and be well versed in using those tools. Your communications toolbox can help you resolve conflicts, communicate through difficult emotions, listen effectively, cultivate trust, and even survive lying and cheating in your marriage.

When things start to get heated you can work to control your physiological fight, flight, or freeze response with a few simple tricks:

- Control your breathing.
- Repeat a mantra to yourself.
- Focus on your body movement and body language.
- Give yourself some physical space.
- Use "I" statements to communicate how you are feeling.

Effective communication is not just about the words that come out of your mouth. It also includes understanding how to use your own body language, how to read other people's body language as well as understanding how your past relationships and how your parents handled their marriage plays a role.

Cultivating and building trust within your relationship is so important and is a key component to a healthy and lifelong relationship. You should always be transparent with one another, talk about your common goals together, be able to give each other your own space, share your common values, and promote a safe environment in your marriage. When trust has been broken it is a two-way street to fix, it takes a commitment from both parties to repair and rebuild trust. But what about keeping a marriage alive and well?

There are five main components to keeping a marriage alive: having a positive attitude about your relationship, choosing loving actions over hateful actions, inspiring each other to build up your relationship, being virtuous and choosing the right choice over the easy choice, and vibrating with positive and constructive energy.

There are plenty of ways to destroy a marriage too, like always sucking the fun out of everything and being lazy. DON'T do these things if you want your marriage to be successful and to thrive. You have to be willing to work for it!

If there is one thing that you take away from this book, it should be this:

Understand the men and women communicate differently and you each bring your own baggage with you. **Seek to understand your partner and practice patience.** It is going to take time to get the hang of being able to communicate effectively and a lot of trial and error. Don't give up on one another!

With the right tools and knowledge, any marriage can be turned around and spouses can learn to effectively communicate with one another. We covered a lot of ground in this book and I truly hope that you walk away from reading this with a newfound sense of determination to make your marriage work.

References

1. Huffpost.com. (2013). *HuffPost is now a part of Oath.* [Online accessed 3 Jul. 2019].
2. Jenkins, P. (2018). *How To Communicate With Your Spouse.* [Video accessed 3 Jul. 2019].
3. Kercheval, M. and Kercheval, C. (2019). *5 Sure-Fire Ways to Cultivate Trust In Your Marriage.* [online] Fulfilling Your Vows. [Accessed 3 Jul. 2019].
4. Jenkins, P. (2018). *Secrets To Positive Communication.* [Video accessed 3 Jul. 2019].
5. Chan, J. (2019). *The differences between male and female communication style in workplace.* [online] Blog.loopline-systems.com. [Accessed 3 Jul. 2019].
6. EnkiRelations. (2019). *How Men and Women Communicate Differently.* [Online accessed 3 Jul. 2019].

7. Wayne, C. (2019). *How Men & Women Communicate Differently*. [Video accessed 3 Jul. 2019].
8. Jenkins, P. (2017). *How To Improve Listening Skills - Communication*. [Video accessed 3 Jul. 2019].
9. Thompson Ph.D., J. (2011). *Is Nonverbal Communication a Numbers Game?*. [online] Psychology Today. [Accessed 3 Jul. 2019].
10. Moore, R. (2018). *Communicating Through Conflict - The Systems Thinker*. [online] The Systems Thinker. [Accessed 3 Jul. 2019].
11. Jenkins, P. (2018). *How To Read People's Body Language*. [Video accessed 3 Jul. 2019].
12. Psychology Today. (2019). *4 Ways to Improve Your Emotional Communication*. [Online accessed 3 Jul. 2019].
13. Jenkins, P. (2018). *How Understanding Body Language Can Help You*. [Video accessed 3 Jul. 2019].

14. Bechtle, M. (2018). *6 Tools for Healthy Communication in Marriage*. [online] Focus on the Family. [Accessed 3 Jul. 2019].
15. Bechtle, M. (2018). *6 Tools for Healthy Communication in Marriage*. [online] Focus on the Family. [Accessed 3 Jul. 2019].
16. Regain.us. (2018). *What Is The Difference Between Love And Respect? | Regain*. [Online accessed 3 Jul. 2019].
17. Gallo, A. (2017). *How to Control Your Emotions During a Difficult Conversation*. [online] Harvard Business Review. [Accessed 3 Jul. 2019].
18. Soars, C. (2019). *3 Communication Tools Your Marriage Needs - iMom*. [online] iMom. [Accessed 3 Jul. 2019].
19. Flood, R. (2019). *5 Communication Tools That Saved My Marriage | FamilyLife®*. [online] FamilyLife®. [Accessed 3 Jul. 2019].
20. Fileta, D. (2019). *The Walls in Your

Marriage. [online] Focus on the Family. [Accessed 3 Jul. 2019].

21. Key, K. (2017). *Communicating Through Conflict*. [online] Psychology Today. [Accessed 3 Jul. 2019].
22. Sweatt-Eldredge, C. (2017). *Five Keys to Good Communication During Conflict*. [online] Psychology Today. [Accessed 3 Jul. 2019].
23. Fabello, M. (2019). *5 Steps Toward Effectively Communicating Your Feelings*. [online] Everyday Feminism. [Accessed 3 Jul. 2019].
24. Ashley, M. (2019). *Trust in Marriage: How to Build or Rebuild Trust with Your Spouse (with 2 Proven Steps)*. [online] Our Peaceful Family. [Accessed 3 Jul. 2019].
25. Paul, R. (2019). *How to Create an Emotionally Safe Marriage Environment*. [online] Focus on the Family. [Accessed 3 Jul. 2019].

26. Smalley, G. (2019). *Creating a Safe Marriage.* [online] Focus on the Family. [Accessed 3 Jul. 2019].
27. Stritof, S. (2019). *Tips for Rebuilding Trust in Your Marriage.* [online] Verywell Mind. [Accessed 3 Jul. 2019].
28. Brown, J. (2019). *How to Rebuild Trust in Your Marriage After a Major Screw-Up.* [online] Fatherly. [Accessed 3 Jul. 2019].
29. Vilhauer Ph.D., J. (2016). *How to Rebuild Trust with Someone Who Hurt You.* [online] Psychology Today. [Accessed 3 Jul. 2019].

www.ingramcontent.com/pod-product-compliance
Lightning Source LLC
Chambersburg PA
CBHW020244010526
44107CB00002B/89